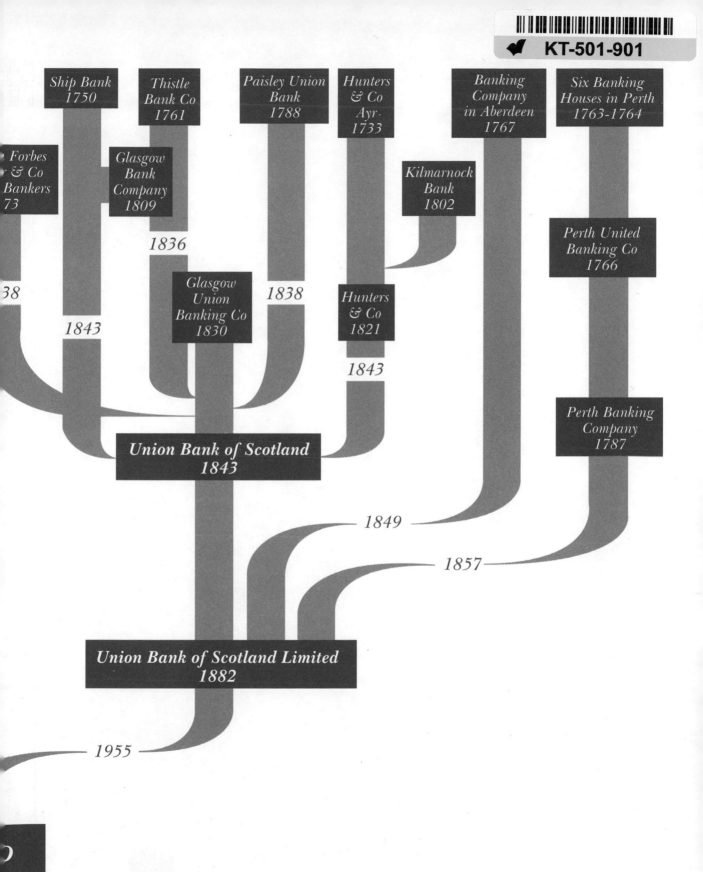

Ship Bank
1750

Thistle
Bank Co
1761

Paisley Union
Bank
1788

Hunters
& Co
Ayr.
1733

Banking
Company
in Aberdeen
1767

Six Banking
Houses in Perth
1763-1764

Forbes
& Co
Bankers
73

Glasgow
Bank
Company
1809

Kilmarnock
Bank
1802

Perth United
Banking Co
1766

1836

38

Glasgow
Union
Banking Co
1830

1838

Hunters
& Co
1821

1843

1843

Perth Banking
Company
1787

Union Bank of Scotland
1843

1849

1857

Union Bank of Scotland Limited
1882

1955

○

BANK OF SCOTLAND
1695 – 1995

A Very Singular Institution

ALAN CAMERON

MAINSTREAM
PUBLISHING

EDINBURGH AND LONDON

Copyright © Bank of Scotland, 1995

The moral right of the author has been asserted

First published in Great Britain in 1995 by
MAINSTREAM PUBLISHING COMPANY (EDINBURGH) LTD
7 Albany Street
Edinburgh EH1 3UG

ISBN 1 85158 691 1

A catalogue record for this book is available from the British Library

Designed by John Martin

Typeset in New Baskerville by Litho Link Ltd, Welshpool, Powys, Wales

Printed and bound in Great Britain by Butler & Tanner Ltd, Frome, Somerset

CONTENTS

At Edinburgh

Our Sovereraign Lord

Act of the Parliament of Scotland of 17 July 1695, setting up
Bank of Scotland

FOREWORD

IN a turbulent and unpredictable world most commercial concerns have a period of vigour, but then the energy wanes and eventually they die or are absorbed by other, newer organisations. A small number of companies survive more than one economic cycle. This is the story of how Bank of Scotland has traded under the same name for three hundred years. The Bank has been visited periodically by 'plague and pestilence'; it has experienced war and peace; and it has survived bouts of excessive rivalry and intrigue. At times the tale is romantic and eventful. At other times the progress of the Bank is frustratingly slow. It is a remarkable story of tenacity and of lessons learned the hard way, set against the social and economic history of the time. I believe it to be the story of a very special company.

SIR BRUCE PATTULLO
Governor and Group Chief Executive
Bank of Scotland

March 1995

Edinburgh from Calton Hill by Thomas Grant

PREFACE

ARCHIVISTS of major banks are in a very privileged position in relation to both colleagues and the public. They are insiders, privy to some of the discussions and decisions which shape their employers' policies, and at the same time observers, assessing the history, character and collective culture of the organisations of which they are part. As a matter of routine, judgment is passed on such matters and on the effects of time and change upon the business. It is small wonder, therefore, that many colleagues feel that the Archivist ought to arrive with the health warning that Robert Burns provided for the antiquarian Captain Francis George Grose, undertaking his tour of Scotland in 1789:

> If there's a hole in a' your coats,
> I rede ye tent it:
> A chield's amang you taking notes,
> And faith he'll prent it.

All businesses are convinced that their own story is unique. Yet precisely what this uniqueness amounts to is difficult to convey in an academic history, concerned as it is to establish long-term patterns of activity and change, and the impact of personality, or changes of personnel, upon policy; in short, the formal history of an institution. Lying alongside this, sometimes as a part of the larger story but more often only touching upon it at particular points, is the informal history, which is probably the part which matters most to those who work within any organisation. This can in turns be pithy, idiosyncratic, funny, boring, frustrating and, very occasionally, tragic. If it is recorded at all, this history merits at most a few lines in the formal record. But it is this collective consciousness (it cannot be called wisdom) which passes down the generations, while the organisation itself sails on, apparently oblivious to the tremors within.

So far as can be judged, Bank of Scotland has always possessed a 'guid conceit o' itself', which has shaped its view of the world in which it operates. This has not been an unqualified blessing. There are troughs as

8 well as peaks in the story and, over three hundred years, not a few miscalculations.

It is inevitable that in the preparation of a work like this many personal and private debts have been incurred. My thanks are therefore due to Dr Richard Saville of St Andrews University, with whom many of the issues were discussed and whose major study of the Bank will appear later in the year. Both of us would be much the poorer without the first-rate work done by our research assistant, Seonaid McDonald, and the calm competence of Sandra Morrison, who typed (and revised) the text many times. My thanks are also due to Win Elliott, whose editing skills and eagle eye have added substantially to the finished result. Dr Charles Munn, Archie Gibson and Michael Strachan have read and commented on the text. Their comments have been very welcome, although I have not always followed their advice. My colleagues Ron Herriot and Helen Redmond-Cooper have shouldered the burden of a distracted boss who must often have seemed 'away with the fairies'. The team at Mainstream deserve thanks for their patience and forbearance on this book. There is, however, a much wider debt which I have incurred over the last nine years: that is to all the members and pensioners of the Bank who were prepared, in informal conversations and in the oral history project, to teach me about the Bank and bankers. Their contribution is incalculable and I can only hope that the present work provides some compensation. None of my work as Archivist would have been possible without the consistent support and encouragement of the Bank's successive Governors, Sir Thomas Risk and Sir Bruce Pattullo, the Treasurer and Chief General Manager, Peter Burt, and Hugh Young, the Bank Secretary. My biggest debt of all is to Alison my wife, and my family. They have lived through the ups and downs of this project with me and sustained me at the low points. For that and much more, many thanks. In thanking friends and relatives (not mutually exclusive categories) for help and advice, it is not my intention to saddle them with the blame for shortcomings or errors in this book. Those are, and remain, mine.

A. C.

Bank of Scotland, Edinburgh, March 1995

—1—

INTRODUCTION

I N 1826 Sir Walter Scott, writing under the pseudonym of Malachi Malagrowther, argued that the banking system in Scotland possessed unique qualities:

> It is not less unquestionable, that the consequence of this Banking system, as conducted in Scotland, has been attended with the greatest advantage to the country. The facility which it has afforded to the industrious and enterprising agriculturist or manufacturer, as well as to the trustees of the public in executing national works, has converted Scotland, from a poor, miserable, and barren country, into one, where, if Nature has done less, Art and Industry have done more, than in perhaps any country in Europe, England herself not excepted.

Even if allowance is made for the propaganda explicit in this statement, the *Second Statistical Account of Scotland* bears eloquent testimony to the changes in the rural landscape and to the increasing tempo of industrialisation throughout Scotland in the period between 1750 and 1820. Scott's purpose was to defend that achievement against over-regulation by Parliament in London, whose intention was to provide a national financial system for the United Kingdom, supervised by the Bank of England. Specifically the legislation included the abolition of the one pound bank-note, whose widespread use throughout Scotland for over a century had been a key element in the move from a barter to a cash economy. There had been no alternative source of ready money in a small and poor country which was chronically short of gold and silver coin

Sir Walter Scott by Sir Henry Raeburn (National Gallery of Scotland)

First Letter on the Scottish Currency by Malachi Malagrowther (Sir Walter Scott)

A LETTER,

TO THE

Editor of the Edinburgh Weekly Journal,

FROM

MALACHI MALAGROWTHER, Esq.

ON THE

PROPOSED CHANGE OF CURRENCY,

AND

OTHER LATE ALTERATIONS,

AS THEY AFFECT, OR ARE INTENDED TO AFFECT,

THE

KINGDOM OF SCOTLAND.

Ergo, Caledonia, nomen inane, Vale!

FOURTH EDITION.

EDINBURGH:
Printed by James Ballantyne and Company,
FOR WILLIAM BLACKWOOD, EDINBURGH: AND
T. CADELL, STRAND, LONDON.

1826.

throughout the eighteenth century. Even by 1825 the move to a cash economy had not been completed. In the year 1833 a roup of the lands and chattels of Archibald McNab of McNab (the McNab), of Glendochart in Perthshire, revealed that of an estimated rental income of £1,300, no less than £500 was paid in kind: in cheeses, bolls of oatmeal, beasts and chickens. The estate was regarded by most contemporaries as old-fashioned and ill-managed (and beyond the Highland line), but the change in the context in which this was set had been very dramatic, and was still within the living memory of Scott's contemporaries.

To Sir Walter Scott, as to the economist Adam Smith a generation earlier, the rise of Scottish banking and its continuing success seemed to depend upon rejecting Government regulation and allowing unrestricted competition between banks. In *The Wealth of Nations* Adam Smith calculated that the whole circulation of money in Scotland amounted to £2 million, of which gold and silver coin provided only 25 per cent. The remainder was in paper money issued by the Scottish banks. Since the Union in 1707 the amount of coin had effectively halved. Despite this, Smith could see all around him evidence of increasing prosperity and economic activity. His conclusion was that unregulated banking was an unqualified benefit to a country. In truth, Adam Smith viewed Scottish banking from the outside and there was a gap between perception and actuality.

The Governor and Company of the Bank of Scotland, founded as a public bank by an Act of the Parliament of Scotland on 17 July 1695, is the original cornerstone upon which this banking system was erected. The story of Bank of Scotland as it exists in 1995 is the story not just of one bank through three hundred years, but also of 21 other banks which have been absorbed over those years. At the time of writing, two – the Union Bank of Scotland (merged in 1955), founded in 1843 and itself an amalgamation of no fewer than 13 partnership banks, and The British Linen Bank (merged in 1971), founded by an Act of the UK Parliament in October 1746 – still make a contribution to the corporate culture, adding weight to the old saying that the whole is greater than the sum of its parts. The story of these two banks will be woven into the story of Bank of Scotland as appropriate.

This history will tell the story of the fundamental part played by Bank of Scotland in creating a banking system north of the Border whose distinctive qualities persist to the present day.

Map of Scotland in 1693

—2—

THE FOUNDATION
OF
BANK OF SCOTLAND

ALTHOUGH it is possible to provide an exact foundation date for Bank of Scotland, in reality the founding Act was the result of discussions spread over several years. These involved Scottish merchants in Edinburgh and London and their English friends and required the active support of the Scottish political establishment of the day. It is one of the more curious ironies of history that while the Bank of England, founded in 1694, was promoted by a Scotsman, William Paterson, it is an Englishman, John Holland, who is generally credited with the foundation of Bank of Scotland. Holland, of whom there is no known portrait, was a paid employee of the East India Company and a prosperous merchant in his own right. He and a Dutchman, Francis Beyer, the Auditor-General of the East India Company, were acquainted with many of the Scots merchants in London, whose interests they supported. Three common threads bound them. First, most of these merchants had been trained in Dutch accounting methods in Antwerp and Amsterdam and may well have been acquainted with each other for over twenty years. Second, a number of them already had experience of working in 1693 with John Holland as partners in a scheme for the manufacture of baize cloth. Third, all had a common interest in the success of the Protestant settlement under William II (III) and Queen Mary and in the peace and improvement in trade which would result. John Holland is reputed to have told the story that 'an earnest and ingeneous friend of mine, a *Scotch* gentleman, importuned me one day to think of a Bank for Scotland . . . so I did'. His main qualification was that he was an experienced and able man

14 of business who was trusted by all those involved.

The bank which they created was unique. It was, and is, the only bank ever to be established by an Act of the Parliament of Scotland. It is the first example in Europe of a joint-stock bank being founded by private persons, to make a trade of banking, wholly dependent upon the capital raised from its stockholders – Adventurers as they are described in the Act, or Proprietors as they have been called since around 1780.

The contrast between the founding Acts for the Bank of England and Bank of Scotland is quite striking. The foundation of the former is contained in a very imprecise clause in a Bill of Ways and Means of the 1694 Parliament at Westminster which indicates that the Bank of England was set up to handle Government revenues. The capital of £1,200,000 sterling raised by the subscribers was to be loaned to the Government to finance the wars against Louis XIV. The Bank of Scotland Act, on the other hand, is carefully drawn up, with a series of detailed clauses for the regulation of the Bank (see Appendix 1). It has to be said that the overall concept has stood the test of time, because the Bank still trades under this founding document. The nominal capital of the Bank was to be £1,200,000 Scots (£100,000 sterling), of which one-third was to be raised in London and the rest in Edinburgh. A Foundation Committee of twelve was authorised, five in Edinburgh and seven in London. The Act specified the books which the Company should maintain for so long as it had a corporate existence (the reason for the completeness of the Bank's archive), but it also included three specific and unique privileges. First, the Company was granted a banking monopoly in Scotland for a period of 21 years. Second, the Adventurers were granted limited liability; that is to say that, in the event of Company failure, they were liable to lose only the value of their subscription, a situation not available to most business organisations until the 1856 and 1862 Companies Acts. Third – and in view of the subsequent history of Scotland, a peculiarity – up to 1920 anyone becoming a Proprietor of the Bank could claim Scottish nationality. The likeliest reason for this clause is that it protected *English* shareholders from prosecution for attempting to break the Bank of England's monopoly, which would have been petty treason.

The reasons for wanting to establish a bank with a strong London presence are not clear, but a number of threads can be teased out. By the 1690s the settlement of bills of exchange, the principal method of financing international trade, was already concentrated in London. Scots traders, as aliens, were at a distinct disadvantage in this market. They were offered less favourable rates than the English and often had to use rival

*Front and reverse of
Scots coins in
circulation in the
reign of William
and Mary*

CHARLES II
A Dollar

CHARLES II
Half Merk

WILLIAM II
Forty Shillings

CHARLES II
Sixteenth Dollar

CHARLES II
A Bawbee or Scots 6d.

WILLIAM II
Forty Shillings

JAMES II
Ten Shillings

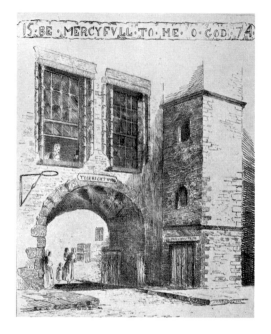

Entrance to the Old Scots Mint

*French drawing of the Procession to the
Scottish Parliament in James II's reign*

English traders as intermediaries in negotiations. A second and more serious reason was that ever since the collapse of the Scottish Mint in 1681 the Scots coinage had been one of the more unreliable European currencies. Between 1660 and 1690, fluctuations against the pound sterling varied between £8 and £16 Scots before being finally fixed at £12 Scots. It was this uncertainty which made even Scots merchants prefer to make their settlements in sterling. The situation within Scotland was complicated by the fact that, while copper and bullion coin in circulation was almost exclusively Scottish in origin, among silver and gold denominations the coins of other European mints circulated as freely as those of the Scottish Mint. Merchants involved in trade wanted security and certainty. Paper currency, in the shape of bills of exchange expressed in pounds sterling, seemed to offer precisely what the Scots coinage could not. A third element was the need for credit facilities within Scotland. Scottish merchants were on the whole 'general' merchants, dealing with agricultural and fishery produce, textiles, trade and cash in equal measure. In the eyes of soured English contemporaries they were little better than pedlars. To be fair, this was not exclusively an English prejudice. In much of eastern Europe in the early eighteenth century *Scoti* equalled 'packman' or 'travelling salesman'.

As suggested earlier, the Scottish economy of the 1690s was one in which goods played as prominent a part as cash. The merchant's minimum requirement was for credit to cover cash flow for the period between purchase of produce and its subsequent sale. This could take months. On his own, the individual merchant was vulnerable to the vagaries of weather, politics and the social status of those to whom he was lending. Collectively, and as a member of a bank in which his liability was limited, he could afford to take a more long-term view of credit and so, with care, extend his operations.

In the generation before 1695 the Scots merchant had operated within Scotland in a very difficult economic and political environment. The Highland war which had been a feature of the first years of William and Mary's reign subsided during 1691. The final act in the tragedy, the massacre of the Macdonalds of Glencoe on 6 February 1692, drew this phase of Scotland's history to a close. Most merchants were involved with participants on all sides of the argument, and part of their necessary skills included knowing (or rather guessing) some of the outcomes. Large areas of Scotland, particularly in the Highlands, had suffered severely from the depredations of war. The Earl of Argyll, for example, needed peace and long-term credit to rebuild his estates – and therefore his income – in order

18   to sustain his political position. The problem for all landowners was complicated by the serious deterioration of climate associated with the 'little ice age'. The whole of Europe north of the Alps was affected, producing from 1695 onwards serious subsistence crises in France, England and northern Germany. In Scotland, the effects on people seem to have been more mixed, and depended upon whether they relied for income on arable agriculture or pasture. Even so, this was the beginning of the period called, in Jacobite propaganda, the 'seven ill years'. Crucially in 1695 and 1696 the harvests failed, and by the autumn of 1696 the price of grain had more than doubled. Indirect evidence of the impact of this near-famine is to be found in the increase in recorded death rates in burghs such as Edinburgh and Aberdeen. But a greater reliance on subsistence farming could not generate the cash surpluses to fund the purchase of consumer goods without a complex network of markets and a ready source of credit.

Therefore, when the sixth session of the Scots Parliament at last turned to economic affairs in 1695, those prepared to support the creation of the Bank did so with a variety of hopes and a range of ambitions: landowners were looking for long-term credit at reasonable rates; merchants were looking for long-term security and the collective strength which could be afforded to them by pooling a portion of their resources and limiting their individual liability; the Scots merchants in London, who appear to have been prime movers in the project, wished to offset some of the disadvantages they faced in competing with their English rivals.

Although the Act for founding a 'publick Bank' in Scotland is the only piece of legislation which has survived from the session of 1695, contemporaries did not see it as the most important business of that Parliament. Measures dealing with moral and religious regulation in Scotland, an 'Act against blasphemy' and an 'Act against profaneness', which were capital offences, were undoubtedly more important, but in the economic sphere the key piece of legislation passed at the end of May was an Act which created the Company of Scotland trading to Africa and the Indies. This Company, promoted by William Paterson, founder of the Bank of England, and supported with enthusiasm in Scotland, seemed to offer the possibility of breaking free from the trading and economic constraints of the previous century. From the first the Company of Scotland, or the Darien Company as it became known, viewed Bank of Scotland as a rival, particularly since, in the shape of John Holland, it seemed to be backed, albeit unofficially, by the English East India Company. This underlying rivalry and distrust is the key to many of the difficulties in which the Bank found itself before 1707.

— John Holland 1658-1721 —

John Holland, so important in the founding of Bank of Scotland, has always proved an elusive figure. His surviving correspondence indicates friendship with the London Scots who promoted the Bank, and his concern for it, even after his immediate connection as first Governor had ended. He came from an Essex sea-faring family whose original home was in Colchester.

John Holland was born in the Bridewell Precinct in the City of London in 1658. More exact information will never be available, because both the marriage and baptismal registers were destroyed in the Great Fire of London in 1666. His father, Philip Holland, was a friend of Samuel Pepys of the Admiralty, and during the Baltic Expedition of 1659 was captain of the *Assurance* on which Admiral of the Fleet Edward Montague (later first Earl of Sandwich) flew his flag.

With the Restoration of Charles II in 1660, Captain Philip Holland lost his command. He tried the merchant trade, but was so unsuccessful that on 24 April 1663 (according to Pepys's *Diary*) he attempted to cut his own throat with a razor. The failure turned him to religion. In 1665, being a non-conforming Protestant, he left England, joined the Dutch, and during the second Dutch War piloted their fleet into the Medway, where it burned most of the English fleet at anchor. It is clear that Holland's sons were still in England, because on 3 May 1668 Pepys records that he went to the King's Head in Islington 'and there by chance two pretty fat boys each of them a cake. They proved to be Captain Holland's children, whom therefore I did pity.'

The family moved to Holland where during the 1670s John Holland completed his education and met Scots merchants. He returned to England around 1681–82 and secured the position of clerk assistant to the Dutchman Francis Beyer, who in 1675 had been appointed Auditor-General of the East India Company. John Holland specialised in accounting for cotton imports at a salary of £40 a year, rising to £60 by 1692. He was reasonably prosperous, and wealthier than his salary would suggest. The best explanation is that he had taken a share in a number of successful East India Company voyages.

In 1687 he married Jane Fowke, the daughter by a second marriage of Walter Fowke of Brewood in Staffordshire. The couple leased Brewood Hall from the Fowke family, possibly for Jane's lifetime, and their three children, Richard (1688), Jane (1689) and Fowke (1700), were born and brought up there. A London house was kept as a business base as John was both a Merchant of the Staple and a member of the London Mercers Company. After his return from Scotland in 1697 he appears to have lived in semi-retirement. He died on 30 November 1721 and was interred in the Fowke family vault in Brewood Parish Church. Jane Holland, his wife, died on 24 December 1740, having been pre-deceased by all three children.

20

Opening pages of the Subscription Books in Edinburgh and London, November 1695, and (inset) John, Marquess of Tweeddale, Lord High Chancellor of Scotland (the first Subscriber), by Sir Peter Lely (National Gallery of Scotland)

—3—

THE EARLY YEARS,
1695–1707

THE first act of the Foundation Committee of the Bank was to place a subscription book in Patrick Steill's Cross Keys Tavern in Covenant Close, midway between Parliament Close and the Tron Church in Edinburgh's High Street. It was open for two months from 1 November 1695 and was supervised by Alexander Campbell, WS, a cousin of the Earl of Argyll, whom Parliament had appointed collector of subscriptions. A similar volume was kept in London. An initial call of 10 per cent of the nominal capital was made before the Bank opened for business in April 1696. Of the total of £1,200,000 Scots (£100,000 sterling), one-third was left in London and its use supervised by a committee of London subscribers, chaired by James Foulis. In the first instance there were 172 Adventurers, of whom 136 lived in Scotland and the remaining 36 in London. A detailed examination of who they were reveals that in Scotland they included 24 nobles, 39 landed proprietors, 41 merchants, 14 lawyers and judges, with seven women subscribing in their own right. The London subscribers included the Scottish Secretary of State, James Johnston, a number of Government office-holders and four officials of the East India Company; the rest were merchants, mostly with strong Edinburgh connections. One of these, Thomas Coutts, was involved in banking in his own right, and the partnership of which he was a member became and remained Bank of Scotland's London Agents until the Bank opened a branch in Lothbury in the City of London in 1867.

On New Year's Day 1696 an office was leased in Mylne Square, near the present-day North Bridge in Edinburgh, and the first official, David

22 Spence, was appointed Secretary of the Bank. His duties involved care of the kist or chest in which coins and bills were stored and the care and custody of all the Bank's papers. The subscribers then got down to the business of electing a Governor and Deputy Governor and appointing a Treasurer, Accountant and tellers. It now seems clear that John Holland's election as Governor was an attempt to deflect the hostility of the English Parliament to all matters Scots. The activities of the Darien Company, to which many of the Bank's Adventurers also subscribed, were the main source of this hostility, and a number of London-Scots merchants narrowly escaped prosecution for treason. Edinburgh's reputation for parsimony is well earned: Holland was instructed to come to Scotland at his own expense, and his salary was settled at 10 per cent of the Company's profits after a dividend of 12 per cent had been paid to the Adventurers.

The first Accountant, George Watson, was appointed to set up the bookkeeping system, and the new Directors drew up regulations which defined and limited the activities of the new Bank. The key clause was the one which forbade the Directors and managers collectively from using the joint-stock or profits of the Bank for any purpose other than the trade of lending and borrowing money on interest, and the negotiation of bills of exchange. This ensured that the Bank would not develop into a general trading company and allow sidelines to dominate its business. Effectively this ensured that the Bank would provide accommodation for borrowers, deal with money transmission to and from London and elsewhere, and discount bills of exchange. It also ensured that the Bank's capital would not become tied up in long-term loans to landowners, a disappointment to many of the original supporters and a continuing source of criticism. Central to these concerns was the decision to issue a paper currency, backed by the Bank's capital, to expand credit and facilitate payments. There were precedents elsewhere for this, in negotiable goldsmiths' notes in England and again in Amsterdam and among northern Italian banks. Scottish bank-notes had to be derived from first principles, which included the establishment of a paper mill on Lord Yester's estate at Gifford in East Lothian and later at Colinton near Edinburgh. Two types of bank-note were issued, both valued in sterling: one was negotiable only at the point of issue and included the name of the payee (the forerunner of the cheque); the other was payable in cash on sight to a bearer who need not be named. The latter could pass from hand to hand and is therefore the direct ancestor of the modern bank-note. The concept of 'legal tender' was confined to coin issued under royal authority. Every note was hand-numbered and recorded, as well as having a 'stub' against which it was matched. After various experiments, the note issue represented roughly

Mylne Square, Edinburgh

*The Darien Kist, the first safe, inherited with the
Mylne Square premises*

40 per cent of the Bank's nominal capital by about 1700, and denominations of £100 down to £5 sterling were used. Local offices were established in Glasgow, Aberdeen, Dundee and Montrose, and a proportion of notes placed in each for local circulation, returnable only to the issuing office.

Loans by the Bank were made on heritable bonds in the name of the individual requiring the loan, usually guaranteed by two 'cautioners'. Loans were also granted on personal security but only up to a maximum of £500 Scots. The maximum legal interest of 6 per cent per annum was charged on these loans. The earlier comment that Bank of Scotland was not a 'Government' bank requires some modification. Many of those granted loans in the first two years of the Bank's existence were the tacksmen, or commissioners of supply for Government revenues. Lt-Col John Erskine borrowed money to pay the troops in Stirling Castle against security of Government payment. The connection, therefore, was at one remove from the Government but it was not entirely absent.

The Bank opened for business in the teeth of competition and faced the first of a series of bank wars which marked Bank of Scotland's history for the first hundred years.

The activities of the Darien Company in London infringed the monopolies granted to both the Bank of England and the English East India Company; so, fearing prosecution, Darien's main promoters, William Paterson (ironically, founder of the Bank of England) and Roderick Mackenzie, fled back to Scotland in February 1696 and immediately opened subscription ledgers. By the beginning of August some £400,000 sterling had been pledged, and the Company held over £34,000 in coin, rather more than six times the amount held by Bank of Scotland. By this time the split between Bank and Darien Company directors was complete, and it is clear that Paterson intended to establish the Company as a bank in all but name, thereby destroying Bank of Scotland's legal monopoly. Loans were made, notes were printed and sums of money sent to London to enter the discount market for exchequer bills. Paterson's supporters treated Bank of Scotland as little better than a front for the East India Company.

Left: *George Watson, the first Accountant, and two pages of the first running cash book of the Bank*

Right: *The first ledger of the Bank*

Grant of Arms to the Bank, 1 March 1701.
The motto 'Tanto Uberior' means 'Ever more Prosperous'

The Bank's second home, above John's
Coffee House, Parliament Square, Edinburgh

Claim and counterclaim are to be found in pamphlets preserved in the National Library of Scotland, in which each side sets out its position. To compound matters further, it is clear that by this time the directors of the Bank of England regarded Paterson as a scoundrel who had betrayed them. During the summer of 1696 the Darien Company's intention to break Bank of Scotland became open. Bank-notes of the Darien Company were placed in all the main burghs, and Bank of Scotland's notes were bought up and accumulated, so that they could be returned all together with a demand for cash. By August Bank of Scotland was in crisis. Bank lending was stopped, and a further call of 20 per cent of the nominal capital was necessary. This was described as a 'loan', and in the event was sufficient to tide the Bank over, accompanied as it was by rigorous cuts in expenses and a strict watch on lending. The major casualty was the branch network, which was closed down. Two events shifted the balance back in the Bank's favour. The political establishment realised that the Government and its friends in Scotland would suffer if Bank of Scotland went under. Secondly, the Darien Company's incompetence in financial matters began to emerge, culminating with revelations in early November that nearly half the subscription had disappeared and could not be accounted for. Most of this had been embezzled, and 9 per cent of the total subscription was never recovered. It was only at this point that the Darien Company began to look seriously at colonisation schemes in Central America.

A Pistole of William II's reign, one-twelfth of all the gold in Scotland won in the Isthmus of Panama

In the event, the Directors' report to the Adventurers indicated that Bank of Scotland had survived, but only just. John Holland left Edinburgh in March 1697; and in the subsequent elections for Governor, the Earl of Leven, Governor of Edinburgh Castle, was chosen, with George Clerk of Penicuik the Younger as his Deputy, while the Londoners re-appointed Francis Beyer and John Holland. Despite the instinctive caution of Leven and his Directors, the Bank had no choice but to increase the circulation of paper, because the crisis in agriculture, accompanied by the outflows of coin associated with the Darien Company's activities, meant that from 1697 there was a severe cash shortage in Scotland which was to last up to and beyond the Act of Union. As might be expected in a period of agricultural crisis, the Bank's loans to landowners performed poorly, if at all.

By 1699 the Bank had moved to premises above John's Coffee House in Parliament Square, Edinburgh, had repaid the 'loan' of £20,000 Scots

28 from the nominal capital, and even managed to declare a dividend of 12 per cent for the year. On 3 February 1700 a great fire destroyed the Bank and most of the property on the east side of Parliament Square. The Earl of Leven and his troops managed to rescue the books, securities and cash, whose loss would have spelt disaster for the Bank. These difficulties were compounded by its first recorded example of forgery of bank-notes. Although the perpetrator was caught and the trade in forgeries stopped, there was not sufficient evidence to convict him. No dividend was paid in 1700, a new bank-note was designed, and stricter controls instituted on their manufacture and distribution. The Bank moved into premises in Gourlay's Close in the Lawnmarket, where it was to remain for nearly a century, and the bill trade proved sufficiently profitable for dividends to be declared in each of the succeeding four years: 20 per cent in 1701, 1702 and 1704, and 18 per cent in 1703.

Bank of Scotland, as conceived and run by its Directors, was increasingly based in Scotland as the English subscribers fell away. Thomas Coutts and James Campbell had both left the list of London supporters by 1701 – although Coutts remained the Bank's London agent. The practical consequence of this weakening of the London link was that the Bank became less attuned to the political situation. A further threat arose in 1702, when James Armour proposed a scheme for a national land bank. He suggested that the Government issue paper money against the capitalisation of annual land values in Scotland. Its attractions were obvious to those who had provided funds for the Darien Scheme and hoped to recoup their losses. A plan to merge this new bank with Bank of Scotland came to nothing, but it made the Directors realise that they needed to do more to support local trade in Scotland. The Bank's answer was twofold: to increase its volume of business in loans and bills; and to issue a bank-note for £12 Scots or £1 sterling. The unfortunate result was that the Bank over-extended its trading. All might have been well had not economic and political events south of the Border seriously affected Scotland. The export of coin to pay for the Duke of Marlborough's military campaigns on the Continent caused a scarcity of money throughout Britain. In the autumn of 1703 a hurricane destroyed a huge volume of Dutch and English shipping in the Channel and wrought havoc along much of the south coast of England. Finally, confidence in the Government fell with a series of military reverses in the war, and all the main London stocks fell in value. The result was that on 18 December 1704 the Bank was forced to stop cash payments and all lending and discounts. This stop lasted for five months and required firm Scottish Government intervention.

The Scots Privy Council, chaired by the Marquess of Tweeddale,

David, third Earl of Leven, Governor of Bank of Scotland 1697-1728, and
Governor of Edinburgh Castle, by Sir John de Medina (National Gallery of Scotland)

30   required that the Bank issue a balance sheet. This statement showed that, in theory at least, all creditors could be paid. The practical problem which was concealed from the public was that this presupposed that all loans could be recovered quickly, which was very far from the case. Most of Scotland's remaining gold and silver coinage disappeared from circulation at this time, and there was effectively a total stop on credit. To compound the situation further, Queen Anne's health gave cause for concern, and the future succession demanded serious discussion between the English and Scots Parliaments. This was Bank of Scotland's nadir.

In this climate a variety of new banking schemes were proposed, but all involved Bank of Scotland being absorbed in a new Government bank. The most plausible and superficially attractive was that proposed in 1705 by John Law of Lauriston. Its essential features were to combine the trading functions of Bank of Scotland with the benefits of a land bank. This project was strongly supported by the Duke of Argyll (as he had become in 1701) and backed by the *Squadrone*, the name usually given to those who were increasingly moving into political power in Scotland and were committed to a Union of Parliaments. Had the project been successful, it would have given Argyll and his supporters total control over the supply of credit in Scotland and therefore the Scottish economy.

For these reasons, all who were not of Argyll's persuasion were keen to see the Bank reopen, and the *Squadrone* over-played their hand. But it is from this date that the Argyll interest was opposed to Bank of Scotland. On the other hand, the Bank's Directors supported the Act of Union because they believed that the agreements contained in the negotiations would lead to an increase in trade and therefore to more settled conditions, which would in turn lead to an increase in the Bank's business. In short, the Union was seen as contributing directly to the Bank's good health.

In its first eleven years of business the Bank had weathered major political and economic storms. It had, moreover, learned a great deal about the business of banking, more often than not by the pragmatic lesson of 'getting it wrong'. The crucial change in its situation by 1707 was that it was no longer run by Scotland's ruling élite and tacitly backed by the Government.

—4—

THE ACT OF UNION AND AFTER, 1707–50

T HE Act of 1707 uniting the parliaments of England and Scotland – in the words of the Treaty, 'An Incorporating Union' – was the outcome of tortuous discussions on both sides of the Border lasting four years. The conclusion, that it represented the only real future for the Scottish economy, was not seriously challenged until the 1970s and the advent of North Sea oil. The benefits and costs of merging the economy of a small, poor country with that of a large, wealthy one has been much debated by historians. The incorporation of the former East Germany into the Federal Republic of Germany in the 1990s has given us a much clearer idea of the difficulties and costs involved in amalgamating two economic systems at different stages of development. Previously it had not been appreciated that, in the short term at least, there could be severe economic strains on the larger partner.

For most Lowland Scots the crucial part of the Act (apart from the Presbyterian settlement of Scotland's national Church) was contained in the financial arrangements of clause XV. England was to pay Scotland £398,026 sterling, with an additional sum, called the 'arising equivalent', which represented a proportion of the increased tax revenue resulting from the Union. The 'arising equivalent' did not arise for almost a generation after 1707 and in itself indicates some of the immediate consequences of the Union upon Scotland. The sums of money were to be used in five ways. Scotland's public debts, which stood at £200,000 sterling, were to be paid. The costs and losses incurred in the recoinage of Scots coin were to be reimbursed, a matter of crucial importance to Bank of

32 Scotland. The bulk of the payment, some £232,884 sterling, was to be used to compensate those who had lost money in the failed Darien Scheme to establish a Scottish colony on the Isthmus of Panama in Central America, and a development fund was to be created to encourage fisheries, textiles and other industries. Finally, the expenses of the Scots commissioners, some £30,000, were to be met. In the event only the last item was met in full, giving rise to the gibe made by Andrew Fletcher of Saltoun, a consistent opponent of the Union, that the Scots commissioners were 'a parcel of rogues bought with English gold'.

For Scottish merchants the crucial outcome of the Union was the removal of disabilities, for example, the English Navigation Acts, which they had faced when competing with their English rivals. For Bank of Scotland, appointment as agent to oversee the recoinage offered immediate profits and the prospect of longer-term benefits from the changes.

The outflow of coin from England to Scotland which these payments

Edinburgh from the north in Queen Anne's reign by John Slezer

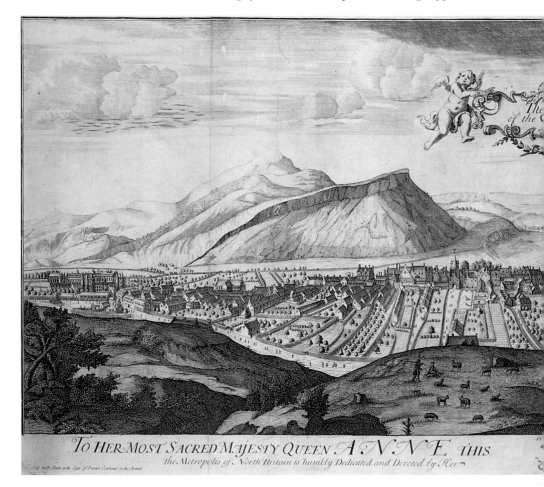

To Her Most Sacred Majesty Queen ANNE this
The Metropolis of North Britain is humbly Dedicated and Devoted by Her

represented seriously worried the directors of the Bank of England. It ran contrary to the accepted economic wisdom of the day. Mercantilism taught that any export of specie (coin or bullion) from a country equalled loss of wealth. There was also one very practical consideration. The removal of coin from England to Scotland simultaneously with the cash requirements of Marlborough's armies on the Continent meant that more Exchequer bills and bank paper would have to be placed with Government contractors. Any military reverse could cause a run on the bank, and the paper itself was unpopular because it had to be held longer before it could be redeemed for cash. The directors of the Bank of England took a decision to attempt to save coin by sending to Edinburgh only £100,086 sterling in coin, making up the balance with Exchequer bills. Effectively a new paper currency was to be launched in Scotland which was designed, quite deliberately, to challenge Bank of Scotland's monopoly and extend the Bank of England's operations in Scotland.

PROSPECT OF HER ANCIENT CITY OF EDINBURGH.
Majesties most Dutifull and most Obedient Subject and Servant

34

Note of the whole Species recoyn'd in
Scotland conform to the articles of UNION

Sterling

16. 8. October 1707 Exhibit to the Lords of Privy
Council of forraign Coyn besides what } £118699..11:2
was previously given in to the Mint

Given in to the mint befor that day --- £13381..6:8

26. The Scots Coyn, called in the 10 Febry 1708 ———— £132080..17:10

20 16 June 1708 Exhibit to the Lords of
Session of Scots Crown, fourty, Twenty } £51856..13:9
and Ten shilling peeces being the 2d
dyet aft the Invasion was over

Given in to the Mint befor that day --- £45000...... £96856..13:9

2. November 1708 Exhibit to the Lords of
Session of Scots four merk, Two merk, } £88180......
one merk, Seven shilling, & fyve shilling
and three shilling six penny peeces

Given in to the mint befor that day --- £54000...... £142180..00:0
                                                      £371117..11:7

Besides this there was in Scotland
of English money the sume of

Also the gold being then in great }
plenty it may be supposed that
there was in Guineas & oyr Gold

So the whole Coyn of Scotland }
at the UNION was --- ---

Nota the Scots coyn in the 2d article above was declared
Bullion at 10 Febry 1708 at which it amounted to about 92000
But at the Invasion the 10 march 1708 it was declared currently
& continued to 16 June 1708 when it amounted to the above
sum of 96856: 13:9

Part of the tactic for forcing Scotland to accept English paper was to delay sending coin north for as long as possible so that coin shortage, resulting from the recoinage, would make exchequer bills seem a reasonable alternative. The added attraction was that Scots, desperate for money, would allow the bills to be discounted at less than face value, ensuring either a profit for the discount business in London or a lower cost to the Exchequer than the sums agreed in the Act of Union. Predictably, this was kept secret from all but the inner cabal of Scots ministers and it was the beginning of August before the money arrived in Edinburgh. The news leaked out at precisely the same time as a rumour was circulating that the Scottish Privy Council had been abolished. Scots refused to accept English paper, and amid riots the Scots commissioners demanded a further £50,000 in cash to settle the most pressing obligations. By Christmas 1707 most of the Darien debt had been paid, and the costs of exchange in and out of London fell sharply. Even so, this left many Scots holding debentures payable against the customs and excise or against the 'equivalent', a matter which was to be of crucial concern to the Bank ten years later.

In the meantime, the officials of Bank of Scotland were dealing with the reminting of the Scottish coinage. The process began in Edinburgh at six o'clock on the morning of 17 April 1707. The Lord President of the Court of Session, Sir Hew Dalrymple, and Bailie James Nairn both presented themselves to David Drummond, the Bank's Treasurer, to begin the process. All the English coin was checked, counted and certified, then all foreign coin in circulation in Scotland and finally all Scots coin. The last two categories were then taken to the Mint in the Cowgate for melting, refining and recoining. The whole process took nearly three years and the final products of the Scottish Mint between 1707 and 1709 can be recognised by the letter 'E' (signifying Edinburgh) under the Queen's portrait on the crown, half-crown, shilling and sixpence. The loss in value which this represented was to be reimbursed by the commissioners of the equivalent, as were the costs incurred by the Bank. By the time the coinage books were closed in 1709, some £411,000 sterling had been dealt with. The fee to the Bank was set at 0.5 per cent of the sterling value and this went straight into the dividend paid to the Proprietors. One unsolved puzzle in this story (but perhaps the Bank was exaggerating) is that the Bank believed it had not been fully paid for the work done. The Directors petitioned the Lords of Session for some unpaid costs, which were granted.

Note in the hand of David Spence, the Bank Secretary, about the Scottish coin reminted into United Kingdom denomination

36   In 1711 the larger issue was taken up by the Earl of Leven with both the Privy Council and the Lord High Treasurer, but without result.

The payment of the equivalent resulted in cash deposits in the Bank, which improved the cash reserve, and it is from this time, in 1708, that rules were devised for the acceptance, payment of interest, and repayment of cash deposits. In March 1708 a French fleet appeared in the Forth on behalf of James III (the Old Pretender) which, although causing a brief run on the Bank's cash, led directly to the system of depositing items of value on security with the Bank. It was a mere hiccup, because the fleet was dispersed by bad weather before it was able to make any meaningful intervention.

The period from 1707 to 1714 was one of considerable prosperity for the Bank, and a dividend of not less than 20 per cent was declared each year. The certainty of that dividend would be curious to an accountant today. It was achieved by the creation of a hidden reserve. Some of this reserve was the Bank's own stock which was released only to those whom the Directors chose to become Proprietors. There were at least two aspects to this. On the one hand, had Bank stock been freely available, it would almost certainly have been acquired by the political interest of the day, which was increasingly Whig and dominated by the Duke of Argyll. On the other hand, the practice gave credence to the accusation that the Bank was a self-perpetuating and complacent oligarchy, more concerned with its own narrow profit than with Scotland's wider needs.

The Jacobite rebellion of 1715 was a major interruption in the Bank's business. News of the Jacobite army's early successes caused a panic in Edinburgh, and the citizens were determined to change their bank-notes for cash. By 19 September the Bank's cash reserves were exhausted and payments were suspended. Immediately the Bank began to call in loans, and those holding bank-notes were reassured that they would be redeemed with interest as soon as possible. Normal business resumed on 19 May 1716 when lending, first on bills, and then on personal security, and finally in 1717 on heritable property, began again. The loss of business for eight months and the interest to be paid on bank-notes meant that no dividend was declared in 1715. The reputation of Bank of Scotland as the Jacobite bank does not stand up to a close examination of the evidence. As with many institutions and organisations in Scotland, it probably had many Jacobite sympathisers, but even now only the Earl of Panmure, a Director and Proprietor, and Lord Basil Hamilton, also a Director, can be identified as having been 'out' in the rebellion. Colour is added to the story by the fact that the Bank's Treasurer, David Drummond, acted as treasurer to a

Left: *Proprietors' receipts for the dividend on their
stockholding in 1721*
Right: *Old Bank Close, the Lawnmarket, Edinburgh, showing Robert
Gourlay's house, the Bank's office from 1700 to 1806. This property
was demolished in 1835*

fund for the defence of prisoners tried after the Rising. Nevertheless, the Bank's Jacobite reputation stuck in London and ensured that in 1716, when its monopoly of banking in Scotland came up for renewal, this was decisively rejected by the Privy Council.

One consequence of the Union of 1707 was to raise the general level of taxation in Scotland and also to introduce many more excise officers to enforce this. The results were the growth of smuggling as a national occupation and something close to an excise war in which the sympathies of the local inhabitants were always with the smuggler. Numerous occasions are recorded in which excisemen were on the receiving end of bloody riots. The best known example is the Shawfield Riot in Glasgow, when the imposition of 2d Scots on Scottish malt was greeted with widespread public outrage; but riots were common throughout the Lowland towns and ports in the 1720s and 1730s. In 1720 there was also a

The Porteous Mob in 1736 (City of Edinburgh Museums and Galleries)

series of food riots which affected most of the towns on the North Sea littoral. In Dysart in Fife over 2,000 people overran both the bailies and the military. The cause was a shortage of meal, which should have been plentiful since the harvest of 1719 had been good. Once again this situation could be traced back to an additional clause in the Act of Union which offered a bounty to exporters, and as a consequence caused a rapid growth in the meal and grain traffic. In this context the ferocity of the Edinburgh populace's handling of Captain Porteous in 1736 is more understandable. The citizens were incensed when Porteous was reprieved for his part in the shooting of protestors who were objecting to the execution of a smuggler. This was not simply an isolated example of an urban lynch mob, but part of a more widespread popular resistance to the new British state. Such acts confirmed the London view of Scots, in Daniel Defoe's words, as a 'hardened, refractory and unruly people'.

Part of the resistance to the exciseman could be seen as a 'class' matter. The repayment of the Government debentures issued in 1707, and even interest on them, depended upon revenue from the Scottish customs, which fell far short of the demands made on it. In the circumstances the resale value fell sharply to about 20 per cent of their face value. From 1713 debenture holders demanded redress from Parliament in London and began to meet on a regular basis in Edinburgh and London; they included the Governor of the Bank, the Earl of Leven. In 1714 Parliament considered all the claims, which amounted to £230,309, and replaced the old debentures with new ones at 5 per cent interest, again payable out of the revenues specified in the Treaty. The need for cash in Scotland was acute and by 1719 around £170,000 was held by London or foreign financial interests. George Middleton, the London banker, Campbell of Monzie and other Argyll kinsmen led the fight for redemption, refunding of the debt or an improvement in compensation. The model they had in mind was the South Sea Company, which appeared to be very successful. (It is one of history's ironies that Bank of Scotland's present-day London Chief Office occupies the Threadneedle Street site of the South Sea Company.) In June 1719 a new compensation and provision for interest payments were made. Administrative control came directly under the Treasury and the whole operation was outwith the jurisdiction of the Scottish courts. In addition, provision was made for the holders of the debentures to form themselves into a corporation. In essence what was achieved was the possibility of a London-based bank with a secure revenue of £10,600 a year based on Scottish taxation. The core of Scotsmen

The Bishop of Down and Connor's attempt to sell his South Sea Company Stock in 1725

Below: *An early bank-note on which £1 sterling is expressed as £12 Scots. This practice continued until 1750*

40   involved, broadly speaking the Argyll interest, were also investors in the Mississippi and Bank of France schemes of their friend John Law.

It was at this juncture that the Directors of Bank of Scotland made a serious error of judgment. Up to this point the Bank had co-operated with the 'equivalent' men and had opposed the Bank of England's attempts to restrict their activities. In the winter of 1719-20, Edinburgh-based equivalent interests offered a merger to the Directors of Bank of Scotland. The details of the scheme owed a great deal to John Law's ideas and little to the careful banking techniques which the Bank had learned. Ten per cent of equivalent stock would be added to the existing paid-up capital of the Bank while the remaining 90 per cent would be exchanged for Bank of Scotland notes. In exchange, the interest of £10,600 a year on the equivalent stock would be added to the Bank's assets to back the note issue. In essence a large-scale convertible paper currency was to be launched, backed only by unredeemable paper, some interest and vague undertakings. Bank of Scotland's unease was compounded by the fact that London speculation in the Mississippi Company and France drained gold and silver out of Scotland. The Directors rejected the offer.

The Edinburgh Society of the Equivalent (simply those people living in Edinburgh who had been granted 'equivalent' money as part of the Act of Union) then formed a project to provide fire insurance, but this was simply a cover to provoke a run on the Bank. In April 1720, notes worth £8,400 were presented with a demand for cash. This was met by calling up another £10,000 of shareholders' capital and restricting discounts on bills of exchange. Again a merger was proposed by the Edinburgh Society and rejected by the Bank. The collapse of the South Sea Company provoked legislation in the Parliament of 1722 which ruled that only six partners were to be allowed in a joint-stock company unless the capital was incorporated by Act of Parliament; but no mention was made of the equivalent, so only a royal charter would be required to create a bank. A tentative proposal to set up an equivalent bank in London was strongly opposed by the Bank of England. However, the Walpole-Newcastle-Islay group, strongly supported by George Middleton, who dealt with much of the finance for the army in Scotland, secured the passage of the charter which founded the Royal Bank of Scotland in 1727. From this time two quite specific rumours about the 'Old' Bank (as Bank of Scotland was known for one hundred years) circulated in Edinburgh, each of which had an impact on the Bank's business before 1740: firstly, it was unreliable from the Government's point of view – that is to say, it was Jacobite and had been unwilling to lend the Government money during the Fifteen; secondly, the

Edinburgh from the west by John Slezer

The Bank's balance sheet, issued on 18 June 1728
in response to forced closure

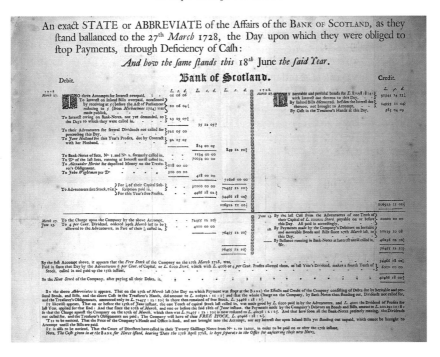

Alexander, second Earl of Marchmont, Governor 1728-40
(Scottish National Portrait Gallery)

Bank was over-cautious and partial in its lending policies. These were restatements of accusations which had been made since 1705 but, in the way of repeated calumnies, the suspicion remained.

Neither the economic theory of the day nor the political situation in Scotland favoured the existence of banking competition. Even before the Royal Bank was formally set up, its agents were accumulating Bank of Scotland notes to be presented in due course for payment. The 'Old' Bank husbanded its resources by calling in its loans and restricting new loans, knowing very well that a struggle for survival would result. Matters came to a head in March 1728, when £900 worth of notes presented by the Royal's agent in Glasgow could not be honoured immediately. Although the cash was found, the offer of payment was rejected because it was claimed that interest was also due. Bank of Scotland suspended payment and closed its doors. The immediate response by the Directors was to look for a further £10,000 of subscription from the shareholders (bringing the Bank's capital up to £40,000) and to publish a pamphlet describing the Bank's history and achievements since its foundation.

In April of that year, George Drummond, Lord Provost of Edinburgh, believing that the 'Old' Bank would be sufficiently chastened, proposed that the two banks should amalgamate. To assist in the persuasion Andrew Cochrane of Glasgow, who had started the proceedings, raised a suit for debt against the Directors of Bank of Scotland until the interest had been paid. The Royal Bank cashier also looked for the arrestment of funds and 'inhibition' of the Bank office, now in Gourlay's Close in the Lawnmarket. As the negotiations dragged on and the Court of Session rejected the legal process, Drummond delivered what he believed would be the *coup de grâce*. He was a commissioner of the Customs and Excise and persuaded the London commissioners that Bank of Scotland notes should not be received as payment for tax or customs revenue. Many local customs officials had already received payment of taxes and customs dues in Bank of Scotland notes. They were reluctant to take the loss if these were not redeemed. In fact, when in late May, early June the notes were presented for payment, the Bank was able to find gold and silver in exchange. The crisis was effectively over.

By July the 'Old' Bank had reopened its doors, paid its creditors and resumed lending. It had survived the onslaught, but the active hostility of Lords Islay and Milton and Provost Drummond was a constant feature of the background to the business of the next twenty years. As if to emphasise its independence of the Argyll connection, the Bank elected as Governor in August 1728 Alexander, second Earl of Marchmont – a man dismissed

44   from all his crown appointments by Sir Robert Walpole, despite a successful diplomatic career from 1714 as minister plenipotentiary in Prussia and between 1722 and 1725 as joint ambassador with Lord Whitworth to the Congress of Cambrai. A number of changes were introduced into the Bank's procedures as a result of its experiences. First, in March 1729 the Directors issued the following statement:

> Now all the money borrowed at interest for support of the company's credit *is paid*, or ordered to be paid off . . . therefore they agree to commence lending at five per cent with the provision: that the several committees shall at each monthly court make a report of what money has been lent out by them the preceding month.

This was accompanied by a series of alterations to bookkeeping practices so that a balance or 'state' could be produced more quickly. Secondly, after the new £5 note issue of 19 November 1730, an option clause was added to

A £1 bank-note of the 1729 design bearing the 'option' clause

The Bank's salary sheet for the half-year ending 27 March 1740 (£250 and eight employed in total!)

the notes. This promised to 'pay the bearer on demand or at the option of the directors five pounds two shillings and sixpence sterling at the end of six months after the day of the demand'. From 1732 a similar phrase was added to the £1 note. In other words, if the 'Old' Bank could not meet the immediate demands for cash of its note issue, it undertook to pay interest on the sum at the rate of 5 per cent a year.

Following the Royal or 'New' Bank's lead, in 1729 the cash credit was introduced, the direct banking ancestor of the overdraft. The first recorded facility was to John Whyte, merchant of Edinburgh, who was granted credit to the extent of £1,000 sterling, with John Craig, WS, as his cautioner. The rules regarding deposits were overhauled and regularised. If interest was to be paid on such accounts, the account was to be for a term of six months at 3 per cent or twelve months at 4 per cent. No deposit of less than £100 was accepted and the bond was to be signed by the Treasurer. Finally, the importance of branches in the main trading burghs was realised and in 1731 a fresh start was made at creating a branch network when agents were appointed in Aberdeen, Dundee and Glasgow. All the branches were unsuccessful, however, and closed within two years.

Despite this, the Bank made steady progress during the 1730s and was able to pay a dividend of at least 5 per cent to the Proprietors. The open hostility between the 'Old' and 'New' banks also began to fade, as each realised that, against the background of a Scottish economy which was beginning to expand, there was room for both to make a living. As in 1720 and 1727 there were serious food riots in Scotland, the result of poor harvests and rising grain prices. In Edinburgh, mobs attacked granaries at the Dean Village, Gilmerton and Leith. The Bank made an interest-free loan of £5,000 to the Provost and bailies of Edinburgh to be spent on poor relief, the first of a number of similar loans it made throughout the eighteenth century.

Phrases such as 'steady progress to prosperity' were shattered by news of the arrival of Prince Charles Edward Stuart at Moidart on 6 August 1745. The Highland army's progress towards Edinburgh was preceded by rumour and counter-rumour and accompanied by many secret hopes and fears. The Directors' reaction to the Forty-five must surely give the lie to the belief that the 'Old' Bank remained Jacobite in anything more than nostalgic sympathy. Quite simply, rebellion was bad for business, and bankers acted, so far as was possible, in ways to protect it. The minute books of the Bank make it clear that great efforts were made to gather in bank-notes ahead of the Highlanders. Roughly 50 per cent of the issue was withdrawn and destroyed between August and November 1745, so that credit was

46   effectively withdrawn from Highlanders. The Royal Bank was not so lucky, and the diary of John Campbell, Cashier of the Royal, provides a vivid account of the consequences of Prince Charles's secretary, Murray of Broughton, having £10,000 of Royal Bank notes in his possession. John Campbell was on the horns of a dilemma. On the one hand, he was required by law to provide coin on demand for bank-notes when presented. On the other hand, too ready compliance with Murray's demands might have brought the charge of colluding in rebellion. On 13 September Bank of Scotland's cash, ledgers, title deeds, bonds and books were moved into the house of Major Robertson – Adjutant of the Garrison at Edinburgh Castle – in three iron chests. One room became a 'safe', which was locked and the keys handed to the Treasurer. In gratitude (or perhaps as an insurance policy) the Bank lent General Preston, the governor of Edinburgh Castle, £10,000 to ensure payment of the garrison's wages.

On 16 September, Prince Charles's Cameron Regiment, under their Clan Chief, Lochiel, rushed the Netherbow, and Edinburgh fell to the Highland Army without bloodshed. The Bank remained closed for eight weeks while Prince Charles's army occupied the city and all business came to a standstill. The Castle remained in Government hands. On 31 October, after the Highlanders had left, three of the Bank's Directors went to the Castle and brought out sufficient cash and notes for business to reopen in a modest way. In January 1746 a duplicate set of ledgers and minutes was commissioned in case of accidents. By March, matters were slowly returning to normal and cash accounts were reopened where good security could be offered. Finally, on 5 April 1746, all the books and cash were brought back to Old Bank Close and the full business of the Bank was restored. The help of Major Robertson was acknowledged by a gift of thirty guineas 'for preserving the cash in his rooms during the late unhappy confusions', a phrase which captures exactly the Bank's attitude to the Forty-five. The main impact of six months' closure on the Bank's archive is to be found, not in the laconic entries in minute books and ledgers, but in the file of letters either complaining about the Bank's closure or attempting to secure payment for sums of money allegedly 'lost' during the rebellion.

OPPOSITE PAGE:
Top left: *Portrait of The Old Pretender attr. to Antonio David*
Top right: *Charles Edward Stuart, The Young Pretender, in 1752 by Cosmo Alexander (detail)*
(The Drambuie Collection)
Board minute book for August 1745–December 1745
Background: *Entry of the Highlanders into Edinburgh, 16 September 1745, by Thomas Duncan*
(detail) (City of Edinburgh Museums and Galleries)

Lt Ferguson's Bank-notes

On 16 August 1745, Lt James Ferguson was leading two companies of St Clairs, or the Royal Regiment of Foot, when they were ambushed 'by a much superior force of rebels' – that is, Lochiel's Camerons. This first skirmish of the Forty-five took place at Highbridge in Lochaber, and Lt Ferguson was carrying the pay for his men – some £59 sterling in Bank of Scotland notes (the 1995 equivalent would be about £3,000). Ducking behind a convenient rock while the bullets whistled over their heads, Lt Ferguson and his sergeant proceeded to destroy the notes, Lt Ferguson putting the numbers into his coat lining while Sgt Johnston mutilated the rest. Both men were captured and paroled, and on 6 September appeared before the Bank directors to reclaim the money due. After a certain amount of discussion, because the amount claimed did not match the numbers in the bank-note issue ledger, the sum was repaid in full and the two men were instructed to join the garrison at Edinburgh Castle.

Private, Grenadier Company
1751
The 1st of Foot (Royal Scots)

Private, Grenadier Company
1742
The 1st of Foot (Royal Scots)
(Royal Scots Museum)

Lt Ferguson's petition

—5—

NEW BANKS AND NEW HORIZONS, 1746–75

IN the quarter-century after the defeat of the Jacobites at Culloden, the banking system of Scotland developed very rapidly to service the needs of an economy which was finally beginning to feel the real benefits of the Act of Union. In one matter Scotland was unique: most of its business was settled in paper currency, issued by one of the country's many banks, while gold and silver coin almost disappeared from circulation. This was commented on by Adam Smith in *The Wealth of Nations*. It seemed to Smith that unregulated competition between banks was the key which opened the door for a small, poor country on the periphery of Europe to 'punch above its weight' (a phrase used in a different context by Foreign Secretary Douglas Hurd) in international affairs, and to improve dramatically on its economic inheritance.

1   The British Linen Company

On 5 October 1746 a third company whose shareholders also had limited liability was added to the 'Old' and 'New' banks by royal charter. The British Linen Company (so called because the concepts of *Scottishness* and *Englishness* were to give way to the Britishness created by the Union) opened its doors in Halkerston's Wynd, Edinburgh, 'to carry on the linen manufactury in all its branches'. It brought together and formalised a variety of interests, including the Edinburgh Linen Co-partnery, which had been concerned with improving the quality of linen manufacture in Scotland in the previous generation. The key political figures were the third

50 Duke of Argyll, Lord Milton (a nephew of Andrew Fletcher of Saltoun, who had fought a duel in opposition to the Union of 1707), the Earl of Panmure and the London banker George Middleton. Work on converting the Edinburgh Linen Co-partnery into a chartered company had begun before the Forty-five, and its managers, William Tod and Ebenezer McCulloch, were convinced that progress of the petition had been delayed by the rebellion. The charter gave the Company limited liability and power to raise a capital of £100,000; however, the trustees decided in the first instance to raise only half that sum. The essential need was to begin business quickly and persuade weavers and linen manufacturers to sell direct to the Company, but also for the Company to employ spinners and weavers without any intermediary. A cash account was granted by the Royal Bank on the security of the shareholding. The overall aim was to raise the quality of linen manufactured in Scotland and to produce a series of standard-quality linens which would be certified and marketed by the Company, thereby making Scotland independent of Dutch and German cloth manufacturers. A subsidiary, and perhaps moral, purpose of the promoters of the Company was to encourage the development of both a widespread cash economy and the habits of regular industry and thrift among working people.

By 1748 the capital had been increased to £70,000 and McCulloch, finding the supply of local flax inadequate, had begun to buy abroad through Scots merchants resident in Riga, St Petersburg, Rotterdam and Amsterdam. One agent, John Coutts of Danzig, was the son of Edinburgh's Lord Provost and belonged to a family which had been trading to the Baltic out of Montrose since the 1670s. The first letter books of the Company give a fascinating insight into the mechanics of linen trade and manufacture, which were controlled from a warehouse in Halkerston's Wynd, off the Canongate in Edinburgh. Warehouses for both flax and cloth were opened in other towns: London in 1747, Glasgow in 1749 and Leith in 1750. To these were added a bleaching green and a cloth-finishing works. The crucial step for the Company's future as a bank was taken in 1747, when promissory notes were issued, inscribed 'for value received in goods'. This is the earliest recorded example in Scotland of merchants issuing notes of hand, and one that was followed shortly by a number of Glasgow merchants. In fact, the offer of trade credit was a necessary part of the Linen Company's normal business. It was also one very simple way of helping to manage a geographically dispersed business which by its very nature relied on small-scale producers with individual spinners and weavers throughout Scotland. This is not the place to detail the ups and downs of the linen trade before 1760, but by 1763 the problems facing the

*Coat-of-arms of the British Linen
Company*

Moray House, Canongate, Edinburgh, home of the British Linen Company, 1753-90

52 Company had become so formidable that winding up the business seemed to many of its directors the most sensible option. One major issue was the fluctuating price of the raw material, flax, which turned importation, at first a profitable part of the business, into a steady loss. There was also the problem of a consistent shortage of ready cash in the countryside. Unlike Bank of Scotland notes, Linen Company paper was payable on demand for cash. New notes were printed in 1763 containing the 'option' clause offering to pay on demand or at six months plus interest. The immediate result was a run on the Company's resources, at one stage to the value of £3,000 a week, which drained its cash account with the Royal Bank. These runs continued to 1767 and could have been much worse had not the Lord Provost of Edinburgh, George Drummond (known to Bank of Scotland from his activities of 1728), instructed revenue agents in the various towns to accept the notes as payment and recirculate them. The cornerstone of a successful note issue was (and is) public confidence in its security and value. In this case it was not helped by growing public differences among the Linen Company's directors. The affairs of the Linen Company were well known to the 'Old' Bank by way of Patrick Miller of Dalswinton, remembered now as the man who first applied steam power in seagoing vessels and as Robert Burns's landlord in Dumfries, but in 1765 as a man with a foot in both camps; and one of the main sources of the runs on the Linen Company was Bank of Scotland, which over a number of years ingathered Linen Company bank-notes and presented them for payment.

Early British Linen Company one guinea note dated 5 April 1768

The transformation of the Linen Company to a bank occurred over a number of years and almost by stealth. Serious attempts at debt recovery were begun in 1764, and the business of granting cash credits (overdrafts) to linen manufacturers was extended to other types of business. From 1765 and the passing of the Bank Act, the banking side of the business began to predominate and the Linen Company advertised that its cash office would be open daily like those of other banks. It must be emphasised that the Company's directors, despite their earlier misgivings, had no intention of abandoning the linen business. The problem was that the few successful manufacturers no longer needed the Company, and the majority faced severe competition from cheaper foreign linens once import duties were lowered and the subsidy on raising flax in Britain was removed. There was one respect in which the Linen Company was different from its older rivals: it possessed the kernel of a branch network, with agents in Forres, Inverness, Peterhead, Aberdeen, Dundee, Dumfries, Eyemouth and Dunbar who were eager to introduce new business.

The Royal Bank recognised the Linen Company as a bank in 1765 and was prepared to support it, but it was not until 1771 that Bank of Scotland was ready to accept its bank-notes and to form a more neighbourly relationship.

2 Banking in Glasgow

The origins of banking in Glasgow and the Glasgow tobacco trade are two facets of the same story – a remarkable historical tale in its own right. The Glasgow merchants trading to North America, unlike their London competitors who tended to act as commission agents, followed the older Scots tradition of buying direct in America, shipping the products to Glasgow and then selling them on. The main product and source of their prosperity was tobacco from Virginia and the mid-southern states. From 1720 onwards, these men were accustomed to providing working capital to cover the needs of trade, but were also prepared to invest in goods, grant credit to planters in the colonies and to invest in port facilities and ships. In short, Glasgow and the tobacco trade were dominated by a group of perhaps twenty families who lent and borrowed from each other to cover the ups and downs of their trade and who could largely depend upon their mutual resources. They included well-known families such as the Dunlops and the Montgomeries, whose social coherence was strengthened by intermarriage. Until recently most historians have argued that there was a close relationship between the formation of banks in Glasgow in the 1750s and the needs of the Virginia merchants for

Glasgow from the east by John Slezer

increased capital to expand their trade rapidly. Although this thesis has now been modified in some important respects, the connection between the two remains clear.

Two of the three banks founded in Glasgow before 1770 – the Ship Bank, founded in 1749, and the Thistle Bank, founded in 1761 – are part of Bank of Scotland's story; the third, the Arms Bank, founded in 1750, is not. All were established as partnerships and in each case the main partners were tobacco lords. The founders of the Ship Bank were Colin Dunlop, Allan Dreghorn, Robert Dunlop and Andrew Buchanan, with two West India merchants, William McDowell and Alexander Houston. The first partners of the Thistle Bank – John Glassford, James Ritchie, John McCall and James Coats Campbell – were all Virginia merchants; only Sir James Maxwell represented domestic interests.

Initially the Ship Bank was seen as a possible partner for Bank of Scotland in the West following the failure to establish a branch in Glasgow. It was launched with full approval and a cash credit of £10,000 from Bank of Scotland in July 1749. The official name of the company was Dunlop, Houston & Co., but it was popularly known as the Ship Bank from the device of a ship in full sail which appeared on all its bank-notes after 1750. The introduction of the bank-notes upset the 'Old' Bank, but an accommodation was reached and they were permitted to circulate. In like manner the Arms Bank, founded in 1750, was supported by the Royal Bank. But by 1752 the two Edinburgh banks were taking fright at the competition which was developing from the Glasgow banks. The breaking-point was the setting up of agencies in Edinburgh by the Glasgow banks to redeem their notes and at the same time to use the Edinburgh banks' notes as part of their reserves. In other words, Bank of Scotland and Royal Bank notes would be withdrawn from circulation by the Glasgow banks and held as part of their reserve, with consequent damage to Edinburgh profits. The outcome was a pact between the Bank and the Royal in July 1752. Each agreed that it would never organise a 'run' on the other; moreover, they would provide mutual support if any third party attempted to do so. Other parts of the understanding covered arrangements for regular meetings (the forerunner of the Committee of Scottish Clearing Bankers), regular note exchanges (a feature of the Scottish banking scene to this day), combined pursuit of forgers, and joint action to make life difficult for anyone attempting to export specie from Scotland.

With their backs secure, the two Edinburgh banks launched an all-out assault on the Arms and Ship banks. Legal action was unsuccessful. The main line of attack was to withdraw credit from anyone who dealt with the Glasgow banks, withdraw the banks' cash credits in the two Edinburgh banks and refuse to honour their bank-notes. The Aberdeen Banking Company, formed in 1747, collapsed in 1753, a casualty in the note war, but the British Linen Company, although resented by Bank of Scotland, was left alone. The simplest explanation for this is that a number of cross-directorships existed; that it had powerful political patrons; and that it was perceived to be operating in a particular niche, which did not represent the same sort of threat as did the Glasgow banks. In fairness, the intention was not to drive the Glasgow banks out of business but to reach a reasonable division which would give room for all. On 18 October 1756 Lord Milton, a director of the Royal Bank, tried to negotiate terms. The Glasgow banks proposed that they would confine themselves to the counties of Ayr, Lanark, Renfrew, Stirling and

A flintlock blunderbuss carried by Bank messengers between Edinburgh, Glasgow and Dumfries

56 Argyll and would not increase their combined capital beyond £120,000 sterling. The counter-proposal was that the Edinburgh banks would open a joint office in Glasgow and would help the Glasgow banks to wind up their operations; alternatively the Glasgow banks could limit their combined capital to £50,000 sterling and trade only in Glasgow, Paisley and Port Glasgow. No progress was made and the two Edinburgh banks appointed Archibald Trotter, with sufficient notes and credit, to harass the Glasgow banks. The tactic, as before, was to collect bank-notes of the opposition and present them with a demand for specie. The Glasgow banks adopted two tactics: the 'option clause' was inserted into the bank-notes; and instead of redeeming the notes in cash, they paid for them by bills drawn on London. The net effect of this in Scotland was the virtual disappearance of gold and silver coin and an almost total reliance on paper currency. It was not popular with the public, particularly when notes were issued for values as low as sixpence, and a number of 'skit' or spoof notes appeared, ostensibly valued at a penny.

Some of the tactics adopted by the Arms and Ship banks were designed to make the collection of cash as tedious as possible. The teller of the Arms Bank was particularly adept at delaying tactics. He would deliberately miscount the money, drop some on the floor so that counting had to begin again, test the coin to see that it was true, and sometimes arrange to be called away on urgent business, which meant restarting the count from scratch. Archibald Trotter, the Edinburgh banks' agent, complained that on one occasion it took 34 working days to count out £2,893, and on another that the daily average never exceeded £36. It was Trotter's patience which broke first and he raised a law suit for vexatious delays. Although he was the nominal victor, Bank of Scotland and the Royal Bank decided in March 1761 not to continue the battle and withdrew their advances to him.

The same year saw the founding of the third Glasgow bank, whose principal partner was John Glassford (1715–83), also a founding partner of the Arms Bank. He was the wealthiest of all the tobacco merchants, and one who is immortalised as the hero of Tobias Smollett's *The Expedition of Humphrey Clinker*. He had a great variety of business interests, as had the bank's other five partners. The connecting link between them once again was the Virginia trade, and the evidence suggests that they were more adventurous, that is to say more aggressive, in their attitude to banking than either the Ship Bank or the Arms Bank, in the latter of which three of the other partners were also involved. The official name of the new bank was Sir Walter Maxwell, James Ritchie & Company, but it was more usually known as the Thistle Bank, after the device which

*Colin Dunlop, Virginia merchant
and founding partner in the Ship Bank*

*The Ship Bank Chest – a wrought-iron and
painted 'kist' from around 1710*

58 appeared on its bank-notes. It began to expand its note issue throughout Scotland, concentrating on the north-east, with a secondary base in Aberdeen. As early as 1763, and just when Bank of Scotland thought the note war was coming to an end, private bankers in Edinburgh became worried about the attempts to push Thistle Bank notes. The Thistle Bank adopted a different tactic for dealing with the Edinburgh banks. As a result, the bank-note war degenerated into pure farce. Archibald Trotter wrote to the joint committee on 9 December 1763, describing an unexpectedly convivial meeting with Sir James Maxwell and his colleagues at the Thistle Bank:

> After drinking a few glasses of wine Sir James Maxwell broke the ice and told me he was sorry on his first acquaintance with me, to be obliged, him, and his company to take a protest against me, to which I answered I know no difference that was betwixt us, upon that Barclay [a Glasgow lawyer] pull'd out a long paper cut and read over. This conduct of theirs was unexpected by me. . . . After that was over Sir James and the rest of the gentlemen insisted on my staying to sup with them . . . and we spent a very merry night together till past one a clock, and not one word of banking passed more . . . Last night's gambol has thrown me back greatly in health today. I wish I was with you to get these troublesome affairs out of head for a few days . . .

Edinburgh was not amused and delivered a sharp instruction to 'avoid like

Two 'Bank' notes issued by merchants – the proliferation of these threatened the stability of paper currency and they became non-negotiable after the 1765 Bank Act

entanglements in future'. One major problem was that Thistle Bank notes became a prime target for forgery and by 1768 a large number of known forgeries were in circulation. It was at least partly in response to this that the cashier of the newly formed Banking Company in Aberdeen refused to accept Thistle Bank notes and thereby provoked a note war in the north of Scotland. The capture, trial and conviction (and hanging) of William Herries of Ayr for forgery improved matters but did not eliminate the problem. The

Above: *Aberdeen from the south in 1750 by Mossman. The Banking Company in Aberdeen opened its doors on 1 January 1767. It became one of the constituent banks of the Union Bank of Scotland in 1849 (Aberdeen City Art Gallery and Museum)*

Right: *A Glasgow 'skit' note for one penny, including an option clause of a song in exchange for interest due*

60   note war had brought the whole matter of the issue of paper bank-notes into disrepute, and an alternative method of regulation was required.

Despite the note war it has to be said that the Glasgow banks, the Ship Bank in particular, prospered. Great profits were to be made supplying and supporting the British war effort in North America, and the end of the war with France (known as the Seven Years War) in 1763 opened vast new areas of Nova Scotia, Quebec and the Allegheny region to settlement and trade. By 1761 the Neat Stock, which we would now understand as net profit, for division among the partners stood at £12,900. In fact the partners consistently reinvested their profits in the business, which in part explains the rapid and secure growth of their working capital. When drawing up new articles of partnership in 1765 the Ship Bank proprietors could record that:

> we . . . find the amounts of debts owing by us to be (including our own signed notes) £127,550: 16s.: 8½ sterling and interest &c. on accounts not settled £705: 18: 4¾. The amount of debts owing to us we find to be £129,702: 14: 0¼d., and interest owing to us on accounts &c. not settled £1,554: 1: 1d. sterling, from which there appears to be a balance owing to us of £3,000 sterling, which is our Neat Stock this 30th of August 1753.

In 1765 Bank of Scotland led a lobby of Parliament at Westminster, and a statute was passed – 'an Act to prevent the inconveniences arising from the present method of issuing notes and bills, by the banks, banking companies, and bankers in that part of Great Britain called Scotland'. This contained three main provisions: bank-notes containing the option clause were outlawed as from 15 May 1766; summary diligence (instant legal redress) was permitted against anyone issuing bank-notes and not redeeming them on demand; and finally the issue of bank-notes for sums of money less than twenty shillings (£1) sterling was forbidden.

The Bank Act of 1765 was in part an acknowledgment by Bank of Scotland that the climate in which it was operating had changed. In summary, by 1770 there were two banks with limited liability and a third, the British Linen Company, *en route* to joining them; and there were three partnership banks in Glasgow, seven private banks in Edinburgh and probably two in Glasgow. In addition, small partnerships had coalesced into larger organisations in Aberdeen, Perth and Dundee, with Douglas, Heron and Co. of Ayr absorbing previous banking operations in Ayr and Dumfries in 1770–71. Part of Bank of Scotland's response was a radical reorganisation of its internal management and structure, effectively the first for over fifty years. The key figure was Patrick Miller of Dalswinton, who became a Director in 1767 and pushed for the changes required. These were opposed by a number of Directors, who were voted out of office in 1771, and some reforms were instituted; the most important was that voting rights would rest with the share rather than with the shareholder. In other words, one Proprietor with 200 shares could not be outvoted by two with 20 shares each. It was also agreed that each year the three longest-serving Directors would retire and would not be eligible for re-election for at least a year thereafter. The paid-up capital of the Bank was increased to £80,000. Perhaps most important of all, in 1771 formal arrangements were set up to provide for a regular and general exchange of bank-notes. Hand in hand with this there developed a system of settling inter-bank accounts on a weekly basis.

Bank of Scotland's policy was determined by the Directors, with all salaried staff occupying a subsidiary role. Responsibility for implementing the Directors' policy before 1772 rested with the three senior officers of the Bank – the Treasurer, the Secretary and the Accountant, each heading a 'department' dealing with a particular aspect of the Bank's business. The Treasurer was responsible for dealing with bills of exchange, inland bills and cash accounts, the vehicle through which the Bank's notes were circulated. The Secretary handled all legal matters, dealt with correspondence and kept the minutes, while the Accountant ran and organised the Bank's bookkeeping systems. The general impression given by the Bank's own records is that its staff structure was stable over long periods of time. Most men entered as clerks and might after ten years or so move on to a higher position or to become a teller, a key position of trust. All staff came from 'respectable' families who were able to offer the Bank security against defalcation. There does not, at this time, appear to have been any formal system of apprenticeship. All members of staff were literate and it is perhaps noteworthy that the porters and messengers were all capable of signing their own names in the salary books. The range of salaries was quite small throughout the eighteenth century, the Treasurer and Secretary and Accountant each receiving £100 to £150 a year, with the Treasurer having a bonus calculated as a percentage of deposits, the use of the Bank house and allowances for 'coal and candle'. Tellers were paid between £30 and £50 depending on seniority, while the Bank servant was paid £15 a year. In every case, salaries were paid six-monthly in arrears. Requests for rises in salary were dealt with on an individual basis, but it was more than common for length of service or merit to be dealt with by a bonus or present rather than by a permanent salary increase.

A LIST of the NAMES of the ADVENTURERS

IN THE

BANK OF SCOTLAND.

FEBRUARY 6th, 1771.

Nota, *That those marked* ***, *are, by their Adventure, qualified to be chosen* GOVERNOR, DEPUTY-GOVERNOR, *or* DIRECTORS; *those marked* **, DEPUTY-GOVERNOR, *or* DIRECTORS; *and those marked* *, DIRECTORS.

A

* Sir Anthony Thomas Abdy of Lincolns-in, in the county of Middlesex, Baronet.
* Sir Robert Anstruther of Balcaskie, Brt.
* William Alexander Merchant in Edinburgh.
* Archibald Arbuthnott Merchant in Edinburgh.
Helen Arbuthnott, daughter of Robert Arbuthnott, Merchant in Edinburgh.

B

*** The Hon. George Baillie of Jarviswood.
Grizel Baillie, eldest daughter of the Hon. George Baillie of Jarviswood.
Elizabeth Baldwin, of the parish of Enfield, in the county of Middlesex, widow.
* James Balfour, son of the deceased George Balfour, Writer to the Signet.
** Thomas Belsches, Presenter of Signatures in the Exchequer.
John Blackader, son of the deceased John Blackader, late of St. Leonards.
* John Blair of Balthyock, Esq;
Mrs. Margaret Blair, spouse to Lieutenant-Colonel William Fullarton-Blair.
Thomas Boyes Writer in Edinburgh.
* Archibald Brown of Greenbank, Esq;

C

*** Sir Hew Crawfurd of Jordanhill, Bt.
*** James Carmichael Writer to the Signet.
*** George Chalmers Merchant in Edin.
* James Chalmer Writer to the Signet.
* William Clarke of Bush-hill, in the county of Middlesex, Esq;
*** George Clephan of Carslogie, Esq;
*** Robert Clerk of Mavisbank, Esq;
*** Oliver Coult of Auldhame, Esq;
** Hugh Craig of Corsartoun, Esq;
* Thomas Craig of Riccarton, Esq;
Capt. William Craig, his Executors.
* Charles Craigie of Glendoick, Esq;
** Laurence Craigie Writer to the Signet.
Andrew Crosbie, Esq; Advocate.
** Thomas Cuming Merchant in Edin.
*** William Cuming Merchant in Edin.

D

Her Grace Margaret Dutchess of Douglas.
*** Sir Laurence Dundas, Bart.
* William Dallas Wright in Edinburgh.
* William Dempster Goldsmith in Edinburgh.
Anne Dewar, widow of George Napier of Kilmahew, Esq;
*** Archibald Douglas of Cavers, Esq;
Henry Douglas Merchant in London.
* David Dundas of Newhalls, Esq;
* Henry Dundas, Esq; his Majesty's Solicitor-General.

E

* James Erskine of Barjarg, Esq; one of the Senators of the College of Justice.
* Martin Eccles, M. D.
* James Edmonstone Writer in Edin.

F

** The Right Hon. James Earl Fife.
* Sir Adam Fergusson of Kilkerran, Baronet.
* Sir William Forbes, Bart. Merchant in Edinburgh.
*** Adam Fairholme of Greenhill, Esq;
* George Falconar Merchant in Cadiz.
* James Falconar of Monkton, Esq;
Mary Falconar, daughter of the deceased George Falconar, Merchant in Edinburgh.
*** George Farquhar-Kinloch, Merchant in London.
Trustees of the deceased Captain James Farquhar.
* Alexander Fergusson, Esq; Advocate.
* Anthony Ferguson Merchant in Edin.
Jean Finlayson, widow of John Porterfield of Fullwood, Esq; Advocate.
* David Forbes Writer in Edinburgh.
* James Forrest of Comiston, Esq;
** John Forrest Merchant in Edinburgh.
* John Forrest junior Merchant in Edinburgh.

G

*** The Right Hon. John Earl of Glasgow.
** David Gavin of Langton, Esq;
** Alexander Gibson of Cliftonhall, Esq; Goldsmiths of Edinburgh.
** James Gordon, youngest son of Alexander Gordon of Cairnfield, Esq;
* Mr. William Gordon, late Fellow of Bennet College, Cambridge.
* James Grant Merchant in Edinburgh. Executors and Trustees of the deceased William Grant of Prestongrange, Esq;
*** James Guthrie Merchant in Edin.

H

*** The Right Hon. John Earl of Hopetoun.
* William Hall of Whitehall, Esq;
* John Hamilton Merchant in Edin.
Mrs. Mary Hamilton-Nisbet, spouse of William Nisbet of Dirleton, Esq;
John Hay of Belton, Esq;
* Willam Hay of Lawfield, Esq;
* Robert Hepburn of Baads, Esq;
*** Roger Hog of Newliston, Esq;
*** Roger Hog jun. Merchant in London.
*** Thomas Hog, Esq; Advocate.
* James Home of Gamelshiels, Esq;
* Dr. John Hope Physician in Edinburgh.
*** James Hotchkis Brewer in Edinburgh.
* Alexander Houston Merchant in Edinburgh.
*** Alexander Hunter Merchant in Edinburgh.

* James Hunter Merchant in Edinburgh.

I

*** Sir John Inglis of Cramond, Bart.
* George Inglis of Redhall, Esq;
*** John Inglis Merchant in Edinburgh.
* George Innes, one of the Cashiers of the Royal Bank of Scotland.

J

* Robert Jamieson Writer to the Signet.

K

*** Alexander Keith, one of the Underclerks of Session.
Mrs. Elizabeth Ker, Widow of James Ker, late Goldsmith in Edinburgh.

L

* The Right Hon. James Earl of Lauderdale.
* The Right Hon. David Earl of Leven.
* George Leslie Merchant in Edinburgh. Montague, Francis, and George Lind, children of the deceased Captain Francis Lind.
*** William Loch Writer in Edinburgh.

M

*** His Grace William Duke of Montrose.
* The Right Honourable Hugh Earl of Marchmont.
* Sir John Mylne, Bart. Lieut. Governor of the Island of Guernsey. Lt. Col. George Moncrieffe of Reidie, his Representatives.
*** Lieut. General Alexander Marjoribanks, in the service of the States-General.
* James Macdowall Merchant in Edinburgh.
James Mackenzie, Esq; M. D. his Executors.
* John Mackenzie Writer to the Signet.
* Robert Mackintosh, Esq; Advocate.
* John Maclaurin, Esq; Advocate.
* Edward Marjoribanks of Lees, Esq;
*** Patrick Miller Merchant in Edinburgh.
* John Monro, Esq; Advocate.
*** Mr. James Murison, Principal of the New-college of St. Andrews.
* Archibald Murray, Esq; Advocate.
Mrs. Barbara Musgrave, widow of John Idle, Esq; late Lord Chief Baron of his Majesty's Court of Exchequer.

N

* James Newbigging Writer in Edinburgh.

O

*** William Ogilvie of Hartfwoodmyres, Esq;

P

*** The Right Hon. William Earl Panmure.
* Sir Robert Pringle of Stitchel, Bart. Margaret and Agnes Pitcairn, daughters of the deceased Dr. Archibald Pitcairn.
* Andrew Plummer of Middlestead, Esq;

*** George Pringle of Torwoodlie, Esq; Advocate.
** James Pringle, one of the Principal Clerks of Session.
* John Pringle Writer to the Signet.

R

*** George Ramsay of Whitehill, Esq;
* James Ramsay Saddler in London.
* William Ramsay Merchant in Edinburgh.
* Thomas Rigg of Morton, Esq;
* Alexander Robertson Writer to the Signet.
Katharine Robertson, daughter of the deceased William Robertson, one of the Depute-clerks to the Bills.
* James Rocheid of Inverleith, Esq;

S

* Sir John Sinclair of Stevenstoun, Bart.
*** Andrew St. Clair Merchant in Edinburgh.
*** Charles St. Clair, Esq; Advocate.
** Col. James St. Clair of Sinclair.
* John Scot Esq; late of Gottenburgh, now of Crigie.
* Robert Scott of Benholme, Esq;
* Robert Scott-Moncrieff Merchant in Edinburgh.
* Daniel Seton Merchant in Edinburgh.
* James Seton Merchant in Edinburgh. James Short Optician in London, his Representatives.
Mrs. Susanna Sinclair, daughter of the deceased Sir Robert Sinclair, Bart. her Executors.
* Andrew Skene of Dyce, Esq;
Mrs. Katharine Skene, daughter of the deceased James Skene of Grange, Esq;
* James Smollet, Esq; Advocate, one of the Commissaries of Edinburgh.
* James Spence, Treasurer of the Bank of Scotland.
* John Spottiswood of that Ilk, Esq;
*** James Stuart, Esq; late Lord Provost of Edinburgh.

T

* Alexander Tait, one of the Principal Clerks of Session.
* John Tod Merchant in Edinburgh.

W

David Warrander Writer in Edinburgh, his Representatives.
** George Warrander of Burntsfield, Esq; Grizel and Eupham Warrander, daughters of the deceased Sir George Warrander of Lochend, Bt.
* James Wemyss younger of Winthank, Esq;
*** Robert Whyt, Esq; Collector of his Majesty's Customs in Kirkaldy.
* Alexander Wight, Esq; Advocate.
* Robert Williamson Merchant in Edinburgh.

Y

* James Yeaman of Murie, Esq;

N. B. Oldest DIRECTORS { Ordinary, THOMAS BELSCHES, ANDREW ST. CLAIR, ALEXANDER TAIT. { Extraordinary, ADAM FAIRHOLME, Earl of HOPETOUN, GEORGE WARRANDER.

John Forrest has been dep. Gov. since 1750

List of Bank of Scotland Adventurers (stockholders) as at 6 February 1771

The next major challenge to Bank of Scotland, and indeed traumatic to the whole banking system in Scotland, was the collapse in 1772 of Douglas, Heron and Co., more usually known as the Ayr Bank. This bank had been formed in November 1769 with a nominal capital of £150,000 and a paid-up capital of £96,000. The Duke of Queensberry, also Governor of the British Linen Company, was elected chairman, and the directors included the Duke of Buccleuch – Adam Smith's pupil – and the Earl of Dumfries. All three were supporters of 'improvement', keen to develop both their own estates and the wider Scottish economy. The majority of the 140 founding partners belonged to the landowning and business classes of the south-west of Scotland. It was a private co-partnery, and therefore without limited liability, but was felt to be very secure because its activities were backed by the land values of the property of its partners. In many respects, though not all, it reflected the land bank ideas of John Law. From the day it opened its doors in Ayr, Dumfries and Edinburgh the bank traded on an almost national scale. Cash credits for development of property were granted easily, which permitted a great expansion of its bank-note issue. One consequence was that the Edinburgh banks contracted theirs, forcing a loss on the Royal Bank in 1771. By the beginning of 1772 it was stated that Ayr Bank notes represented two-thirds of the note circulation in Scotland. This note issue was backed by short-term credits from London bankers at substantial premiums. Many of the cash credits were spent on speculation, and the bank found itself over-extended and over-trading. A system developed of borrowing on bills in London to meet bills due. By banking standards it was a recipe for disaster, particularly since few of the directors of the bank had any real banking experience, and the reality was deliberately hidden from the shareholders by the managers. Essentially, the bank committed the cardinal banking sin of lending long-term and covering this with short-term borrowing on the commercial money market. In June 1772 the liabilities of the company amounted to about £1,120,000 and the assets stood at £409,079 in bills of exchange and £827,963 in loans. Roughly half of these loans were to the Ayr Bank's own partners. At this point the London-based bank of Neale, James, Fordyce and Downe collapsed owing some £243,000. Others followed, and in the crisis Scottish paper was heavily discounted, particularly since the Bank of England would not touch it. In fairness, the collapse of confidence in 1772 was part of a Europe-wide problem, and demands upon the Bank of England for loans and cash appeared from all sides. A large number of the Edinburgh private banks failed and there was a panic. Ayr Bank notes were returned to the bank with demands for cash.

64   The two dukes led a deputation to the Bank of England to ask for a loan on the security of their lands. A sum of £300,000 was offered but the terms were so severe that the Ayr Bank felt it had no choice but to refuse. An approach to Bank of Scotland and the Royal Bank for loans of £50,000 was also rejected. They had borne the brunt of the Ayr Bank's activities and such a loan would have severely strained their own resources. The crisis spread to Glasgow, and Bank of Scotland granted loans of £10,000 to each of the Arms, Thistle and Ship banks and ordered up a supply of coin from London. This was vitally necessary to prevent a collapse of confidence in banks throughout Scotland. In other words, it was enlightened self-interest.

Clearing up the mess fell on the two chartered banks, which decided to accept Ayr Bank notes on the landed security of its proprietors. Basically, the two dukes and other partners had to raise loans on their estates to pay off their debts, a burden which some families were still repaying some sixty years later. In 1788 the owner of a £500 share not only forfeited that, but was liable in addition for some £2,200 of the bank's debts. Of the eventual 226 partners in the Ayr Bank in 1772 it is estimated that 114 became bankrupt. As a result, estates were split up and one estimate suggests that £750,000 of landed property changed hands. Much of this was concentrated geographically. One consequence was a great change in the pattern of land ownership in Ayrshire, Kirkcudbrightshire and Dumfries.

Scotch Money: an English lampoon on the collapse of the Ayr Bank

It goes without saying that paper currency on the Scottish pattern was viewed with immense suspicion and distrust in London (a view which over two hundred years of success since then has not entirely eliminated).

The Ayr Bank experience taught the banks two important lessons. First, that despite their comparatively limited resources the two Edinburgh chartered banks acting together could in practice operate as a quasi-reserve bank for the whole Scottish system, and therefore could discipline the more aggressive new banks. Second, each realised that it was undercapitalised for Scotland's requirements. In 1774 an Act of Parliament permitted Bank of Scotland to double its authorised capital to £200,000. This was called up and available by the beginning of 1775. For one observer of the Ayr Bank disaster the years between 1772 and 1775 were spent reflecting and writing about what he had observed. Adam Smith's *The Wealth of Nations* appeared in 1776.

Auld Robin Carrick of the Ship Bank

—6—
TWO CITIES; TWO BANKERS

FOR much of the last quarter of the eighteenth century two bankers, one from Glasgow and one from Edinburgh, came to epitomise the banking practices and attitudes of their own cities. They shared three essential characteristics: honesty, scrupulous attention to detail in all business dealings, and success. And both were remembered in anecdote and literature long after their deaths. For once Glasgow had a slight seniority, if only in the matter of birth date.

Robert or (as he was more usually known) Robin Carrick was manager of the Ship Bank in Glasgow from 1775 to 1821 and his portrait now hangs in Glasgow Chief Office of Bank of Scotland. He was born in Houston, Renfrewshire, in 1737, the fourth son of Robert Carrick, a minister, and Margaret Paisley. The father had been tutor to Andrew Buchanan of Drumpellier, one of the founders of the Ship Bank, and it was in 1752, a year after its foundation, that Robin was appointed clerk at a salary of £25 a year. He was just 14. Six years later, in 1758, he became accountant at £70 a year, and subsequently cashier. By 1760 he was also in business on his own account under the name of Brown, Carrick and Company, which was allowed a cash credit of £990 from the Ship Bank. He became a partner in the second co-partnery of the Ship Bank in 1775, the year in which the Clyde was dredged. This allowed ships which previously had to unload at Greenock or Port Glasgow passage up to the Broomielaw in the city centre for the first time. It was also the year in which the American War of Independence started. The tobacco trade and the tobacco lords suffered a severe decline, but by way of consolation Glasgow's trade to the West Indies improved, bringing cotton,

68   rum and molasses into the city and creating a new business area just west of the old High Street, between Ingram and Jamaica Streets – the district now known as the Merchant City. One of Robin Carrick's first steps was to move the bank office to the corner of Glassford Street, a building which some thirty years previously had housed the Young Pretender. The windows were

GLASGOW HERALD, MONDAY, FEBRUARY 23, 1903.

AN OLD GLASGOW LANDMARK.

THE SHIP BANK BUILDING.

The quaint old tenement at the corner of Bridgegate and Saltmarket, known as the "Old Ship Bank Building"—having housed the Ship Bank for 25 years from 1750—is about to be removed to allow for the widening of Bridgegate; and it is interesting to learn that the Improvements Committee has offered it to the Parks Committee for re-erection in one of the Parks. Early in the thirties, this dwelling was known as Coulter's House; and it was said that here Cromwell convened a Parliament. An inscribed stone, which formerly marked the height of the great river flood of 12th March, 1782, on Silvercraig's Land, a building which stood on the east side of Saltmarket, may be seen on the wall of the Old Ship Bank, where it was inserted for preservation. The house has been described in the Corporation as "a monument of ugliness"—but it is just a few hundred such "ugly" buildings which go to make up the picturesque streets Glasgow people admire in other cities. The desire of the Improvements Committee to preserve, as far as possible, the old landmarks should have the support of the citizens; and if a use can be found for this example of the early domestic architecture of Glasgow, it should certainly be rebuilt in, or near, the Green.

strengthened by iron bars so that its external appearance was 'not unlike a county jail'. There are many descriptions of the interior but there was little (in that generation of Glaswegians) for mere show:

> On entering the rather dark lobby from Argyle Street a passage led to the right, at an acute angle into the business rooms of which there were two on opposite sides . . . the one room looked into Argyle Street and had a small low counter, behind which stood a teller . . . like a grocer's shopman. The room opposite contained the élite of the establishment . . . everything was, as it were, defended from the public; and people transacting business had to stand almost on tiptoe to look over the high wooden screen, with a narrow shelf on the top, which separated them from the bank employes [sic], and bawl out what was wanted . . .

Business was transacted methodically, and slowly, and any customer wanting a bill honoured had to wait while it was taken to 'Auld Robin' for approval. The rejection phrase 'it's no convenient' became so well known in Scottish banking circles that in the Kilmarnock Banking Company it was actually printed on bill rejection slips. One other trick of Robin's was to mark the corner of a rejected bill with his thumb-nail so that if it ever reappeared he would know it instantly. One rejected customer refused to take the bill back and said, 'Na, na, it maun be discounted noo. Ye ken naebody will tak it wi' the deil's mark on it.' The stark and forbidding nature of Auld Robin and his bank produced a sense of awe and apprehension in those fated to do business with him. In later life his very appearance was old-fashioned and strange:

> He was usually attired in a brown-coloured coat, queerly made, with deep flaps on the outside pockets, the broad skirts reaching nearly down to his heels, and adorned with large brass buttons; drab knee-breeches; a striped woollen waistcoat of hotch-potch tinge . . . white neckcloth, with longish ends; white worsted stockings and buckles in his shoes; while a small brown wig covered the pate of this singular looking but able old financier.

The success of his methods is abundantly clear from the Ship Bank records. Balance sheet totals of 1777, which showed £120,352 in the books, had risen to £346,638 in 1792 and stood at £1,028,456 10s. in 1821, the year of Robin Carrick's death. The partnership's profits fluctuated from £6,000 to £12,600 in 1818, the year in which the capital stock of the partnership stood at £67,695, which translates into a yield of 18 per cent at a time when the Proprietors of Bank of Scotland were securing an ordinary dividend of 9 per cent. The core of the business was

70 bank-note issue and bill-discounting. In both, the policy was, in banking terms, conservative. It was precisely for this reason that the Ship Bank was able to weather the economic crisis of 1793 caused by the outbreak of war with France. Similarly in 1797, when the Bank of England was forced to close its doors, the Ship was able to maintain its customers' credit. A printed list of borrowers in 1789 mentions eighty firms or people, reflecting the full range of Glasgow's business and commercial interests at that time.

Robin Carrick's business interests were widespread and included linen drapery and manufacturing such as muslin production. It has been estimated that his personal fortune amounted to half a million pounds, much of which was invested in landed property, the core being an estate at Mount Vernon, where he had a country house. He was a bachelor and usually lived above the bank, but during the summer he tended to live in the country and travelled daily to town:

> Two plough horses composed his whole stud, and most leisurely was their sombre pace much like a funeral pageant. The millionaire banker sat in his carriage surrounded with baskets of all kinds of vegetables in their seasons, and when he extricated himself from the verdant mass, his equerry John Culbertson drove the carriage slowly by way of Argyle Street to the Green Market, then in Candleriggs. He there deposited the contents with the greengrocer, and had faithfully to account for the sales to his master.

His personal frugality extended to his domestic arrangements, which were presided over by his niece, Jenny Paisley. It must not be thought that Robin lived meanly, however. The bank house was handsomely furnished and there were occasional parties. Some of the food for these dinners was taken on 'sale or return', and Miss Paisley had no hesitation in returning uneaten cheeses or fruit to the suppliers. Some of the anecdotes about Robin are recorded in Peter Mackenzie's *Reminiscences of Glasgow and the West of Scotland* (1865), and many may be apocryphal. They tend to centre on his public stinginess, for which there is ample objective evidence, and on attempts to 'put one over on him', for which there is none. There is the story of a prosperous young man about town who presented a bill for payment which was for a large sum of money. It was 'no convenient'. One of his other customers protested, 'Oh you need not hesitate about him, Mr Carrick, for he has started, and keeps his carriage.' 'Oh aye,' said Robin, 'but the question wi' me is, can he keep his legs?'

When Robin Carrick died in 1821 the capital stock of the Ship Bank stood at £91,859. When Auld Robin's portion of £47,695 was withdrawn, the Ship

Bank itself lost its driving force, amalgamating in 1836 with the more recently formed Glasgow Bank Company to create the Glasgow and Ship Bank. In fact, it has been shown that by the 1820s the days of partnership banks like the Ship Bank were numbered. The future of banking lay with large joint-stock banks, which had a much larger capital base.

Robin's Edinburgh contemporary was Sir William Forbes of Pitsligo (1739-1806), who inherited his baronetcy and very little else when his father died in 1743. A baronetcy of Nova Scotia conferred few real advantages since it had been devised as one of James VI and I's money-making ploys, and the actual land had been part of French Canada since 1641. Initially Sir William was brought up in Aberdeen in the Episcopalian tradition – one which was closely associated with Jacobitism. His great-uncle Alexander, fourth Lord Forbes of Pitsligo, raised a regiment for Charles Edward Stuart in the Forty-five and paid the price in hiding, exile and forfeiture. In 1753 the widowed Lady Forbes moved to Edinburgh and through a friend of his father the young William secured a place as a clerk in the counting house of Coutts Brothers & Company in Parliament Square. As the years passed, he became an active member of all the city's

Ship Bank £1 note, 1828 design

72 societies for literature, thought and improvement and a generous friend to all those who from 1760 onwards made Edinburgh 'a hotbed of genius' and a centre of the European Enlightenment. In 1773, aged just 34, he was introduced to Dr Johnson by James Boswell at the beginning of their great tour of the Highlands and Islands of Scotland. Boswell's comments on Forbes are remarkable:

> . . . a man of whom too much good cannot be said: who with distinguished abilities and application in his profession of a banker, is at once a good companion, and a good christian; which I think is saying enough. Yet it is but justice to record, that once, when he was in dangerous illness, he was watched with the anxious apprehension of a general calamity; day and night his house was beset with affectionate inquiries; and upon his recovery, *te deum*, was the universal chorus from the *hearts* of his countrymen . . .

Given James Boswell's reputation, it would be easy to dismiss the portrait as mere flattery. However, since the first edition of *Journal of a Tour to the*

Sir William Forbes of Pitsligo Bt by Sir Henry Raeburn

Unissued twenty shilling note from Forbes, Hunter & Co

Hebrides was published in 1785, and the traits of character are repeated by others throughout Sir William Forbes's life, it would seem to be correct in all its essentials. The main source of information about his bank is an autobiographical essay which Sir William wrote for the instruction of his eldest son, also William, and which gives many insights into the business of a private bank.

The firm which Sir William joined in 1754 was known as Coutts Brothers & Company, the main partners being the four sons of Provost John Coutts of Edinburgh, who had died in 1749. The eldest and youngest brothers took over the London business and under the tutorship of Thomas Stephen developed a profitable banking business, the ancestor of the London bank which still bears the name Coutts. The middle brothers, James and John, were minors, and the Edinburgh house was supervised by Archibald Trotter, whose later career is mentioned in the previous chapter. A large part of the business depended on corn trading and import and export business. In some years it made great profits, in others, losses.

In 1761 the death of John Coutts left the Edinburgh part of the business without a resident member of the Coutts family. So although a new partnership agreement was drawn up among the remaining Edinburgh partners, which included Sir William as a partner, the firm retained the name of Coutts & Co. The new partners resolved to confine their business to taking deposits, granting loans, discounting bills and dealing on the exchanges of London, Rotterdam and Paris. In 1773 the name of the bank

74 was changed to Sir Wm Forbes, James Hunter & Company. Then, diversifying from its purely financial role, it secured the exclusive contract for supplying Virginia tobacco to France. Distribution in France was a government monopoly and the supply was routed through Glasgow. This trade lasted formally until 1778, when war broke out between Britain and France, but it had been in steep decline after 1775, when the beginning of the American War of Independence closed down the Virginia trade.

The key to the bank's success was its care and prudence, of which the autobiography gives many instances. Throughout the 1770s and up to the end of the American War of Independence (1783), the bank invested steadily in Government stock, primarily Navy and exchequer bills. Many of the purchases were made when stock prices were low and resold when prices rose at the end of the war. This greatly increased the personal fortune of Sir William and permitted the bank to exchange a cash credit with the Royal Bank into deposits of £20,000 and to hold a further £20,000 of Royal Bank notes as a reserve. Sir William was always careful not to offend either Bank of Scotland or the Royal Bank, and he gave ample warning of changes of policy. In 1782 the partnership began to issue bank-notes and faced none of the problems of acceptance which others experienced. It is a measure of the stature of Sir William Forbes that during the bank crises of 1793 and 1797 he was automatically included by the two banks in their discussions.

It is, however, for his foresight, energy and charity that he truly lived up to his family motto, 'Neither timidly nor rashly'. He was a founder member of both the Society of Antiquaries of Scotland (1780) and the Royal Society of Edinburgh (1783). He was among those who entertained the young Ayrshire poet Robert Burns on his first visit to Edinburgh. New Pitsligo in Aberdeenshire is a planned village and a monument to his desire for agricultural improvement, while the Episcopal Church of St Paul and St George, in Edinburgh's York Place, owes its existence to the benefactions which arose out of his loyalty to his origins. Edinburgh's Blind Asylum, Morningside Lunatic Asylum, the High School and the Merchant Company were all supported by him. Perhaps most interestingly of all, his eldest son William and Walter Scott were school and university friends, a friendship which cooled only temporarily in 1797 when both pursued Williamina Belches, heiress to the Fettercairn estates, and Walter Scott lost.

It was Walter Scott who provided the most eloquent epitaph when Sir William died in 1806. The lines are to be found in the introduction to the fourth canto of *Marmion*.

Scarce had lamented Forbes paid
The tribute to his Minstrel's shade,
The tale of friendship scarce was told,
Ere the narrator's heart was cold –
Far may we search before we find
A heart so manly and so kind!
But not around his honoured urn
Shall friends alone and kindred mourn;
The thousand eyes his care had dried,
Pour at his name a bitter tide;
And frequent falls the grateful dew,
For benefits the world ne'er knew.
If mortal charity dare claim
The Almighty's attributed name,
Inscribe above his mouldering clay,
'The widow's shield, the orphan's stay'.
Nor, though it wake thy sorrow, deem
My verse intrudes on this sad theme;
For sacred was the pen that wrote,
'Thy father's friend forget thou not'.
And grateful title may I plead
For many a kindly word and deed,
To bring my tribute to his grave:-
''Tis little – but 'tis all I have'.

The phrase 'A shield and stay' was in due course adopted as the motto on the coat of arms of the Union Bank of Scotland, the inheritor of the traditions and businesses of both Robin Carrick and Sir William Forbes, two men who epitomised the creative tension of style and substance which still characterises the Edinburgh-Glasgow debate in Scotland – but reversing the usual stereotypes.

Henry Dundas, first Viscount Melville, Governor 1790-1811, by Sir Henry Raeburn

—7—

FROM AYR BANK
TO WATERLOO,
1775–1815

THE thirty years from 1775 to 1805 saw Bank of Scotland at the then zenith of its power and influence over the banking system in Scotland. The system, and we must call it that, developed rapidly during the 1770s and '80s. In part this was the direct response of Scotland's political élite to the Ayr Bank disaster and the resultant need to provide an underlying stability for banking in Scotland. In part it was the result of providing capital for both industrial and agricultural development. This was in turn influenced by the American War of Independence (1775–83) and then by the French Wars of the 1790s. It is a measure of the success of the strategy that in 1793 the London banker Thomas Coutts could refer to Bank of Scotland as the Scots National Bank without irony or parentheses.

The major element of the story is political, a core part of the way in which Henry Dundas (later first Viscount Melville) managed to weld a variety of interests in Scotland into a solid political platform for the North-Pitt Tory administration in London. The corollary of this is that, with the waning of Melville's political influence after 1805, Bank of Scotland was forced into a more modest role, one for which it was ill-equipped and which carried with it the additional problem of being tagged as the Tory landowners' bank.

The banking system was built between 1774 and 1778. It involved Bank of Scotland and the Royal Bank adopting, in close co-operation, the joint role of a quasi-reserve bank for Scotland. This did not prevent the entry of new provincial partnership banks; however, it did ensure that their ability to trade depended in the last resort upon their acceptance by Edinburgh,

78 and that in turn depended upon the new banks' acceptance of constraints on trading and note issue. It worked, precisely because the system permitted itself to expand rapidly enough to accommodate the financial needs of the expanding economy of Scotland. However, it would be difficult to argue that Scotland at this time possessed an unregulated banking system, as has been suggested by a number of twentieth-century free market economists.

Henry Dundas was the fourth son of Lord President Robert Dundas of Arniston, a family which had a long lineage as Edinburgh lawyers. Admitted to the Faculty of Advocates in 1763, he became Solicitor-General in 1766 and a Director (like his father before him) of Bank of Scotland in 1768. There is evidence that when the young Duke of Buccleuch returned from his continental tour, with Adam Smith as his tutor, Dundas had encouraged his participation in the Ayr Bank. Despite this, the two became friends and in 1774 Dundas was selected as MP for Midlothian, a seat in Buccleuch's gift. It is worth pointing out that Scotland's 36 parliamentary seats had a grand total of 2,660 voters, an average of 74 voters per seat. In 1775 Dundas was appointed Lord Advocate, an appointment which ensured that all Scottish parliamentary business passed through his hands and which by 1778, with the support of the Duke of Buccleuch allowed him to determine the choice of MPs in 25 out of the 36 Scottish seats in Parliament.

Within Bank of Scotland Dundas found willing allies. He supported the Governor, Henry, third Earl of Marchmont; the Deputy Governor, David, Earl of Leven; and Patrick Miller of Dalswinton, to push through the changes which Miller felt were necessary in 1771–72. The relationship between Dundas (Deputy Governor 1779–89, Governor 1790–1812) and Patrick Miller (Deputy Governor 1790–1812) seems to have been particularly close. The evidence of the minute books suggests that during the period up to 1793 this pair effectively decided the Bank's strategy with Miller supervising its execution. The Extraordinary Directorships of the Bank were used to ensure that there was little dissent. By 1775 the Duke of Buccleuch, who because of his parliamentary patronage saw himself as 'prime minister' of Scotland, and the Earls of Lauderdale, Panmure, Dalhousie and Hopetoun had all been added to the Board.

The target of this group in the 1770s was the lesser lairds, made prosperous by Government contracts after the Forty-five, who in the 1760s were Whigs and whose power was personified by Lawrence Dundas of Kerse, Governor of the Royal Bank of Scotland after 1764. The manner in which he was replaced in 1778 as Governor of the Royal by the Duke of

Buccleuch is not entirely clear, but it is known that it involved a complicated series of share transactions in 1775–76 which resulted in some 40 per cent of the Royal Bank's shares changing hands. A proportion of these transactions were a direct result of bankruptcies following the Ayr Bank collapse, but it is certain that a number of Edinburgh private banks, notably Sir William Forbes, James Hunter & Co., Mansfield, Ramsay & Co. (in which Patrick Miller was a partner), William Cuming and Thomas Kinnear were all active in buying Royal Bank stock which they then held as part of their reserve. In addition, several Bank of Scotland Directors (including the ubiquitous Patrick Miller) were directly involved in purchases. The upshot was that by 1777 Henry Dundas commanded a majority of Royal Bank shares, and the elections of 1778 completed the process with a change of Governor, Deputy Governor and six Directors.

From 1776 the thrust of Henry Dundas's policy towards the banks was public knowledge, and during the 1778 elections for Royal Bank directorships it was explicitly stated that, while it was important that the banks should co-operate on a larger scale than before, they would not be united formally into a single bank. Henceforth the two banks marched in step, with clearly delineated activities and spheres of influence, and the senior officials of each met regularly to iron out any differences which might have arisen. At a practical level, interest rates, regular exchanges of bank-notes, balances of notes held by each, the grant of facilities to provincial banking partnerships, and information about fraud and forgery were shared and acted upon in concert. The clear message which was sent to London was that the Government party in Scotland was supported by the most sophisticated and stable banking system in Europe and that there was no place for the Bank of England.

A simple measure of the pace of change in Scotland's economy is that between 1774 and 1804 the authorised capital of Bank of Scotland was raised from the £100,000 which had served since 1695 to £1.5 million by four separate Acts of Parliament, the last figure proving sufficient until 1873. The Proprietors' return on capital never fell below 6 per cent between 1775 and 1815. Between 1781 and 1790 it stood at 8.3 per cent and in 1799 an additional bonus of £90,000 was divided among them. Throughout the period, the Bank's stock found a ready market and shares traded well above their nominal value.

In most respects the fortunes of the Royal Bank of Scotland paralleled those of Bank of Scotland, but the third chartered bank, the British Linen Company, was on the sidelines. After an abortive attempt in 1781 to increase its capital from £100,000 it concentrated on steadily improving its

80   existing business and on developing its local agencies, the earliest of which was probably Aberdeen, started in 1760.

Even a cursory glance at Bank of Scotland's ledgers demonstrates the great variety of projects and industries to which loans were made. There were two main methods of lending: the bill of exchange, which was in effect a loan with a fixed term; and the cash credit – what we would now call an overdraft. The bill of exchange business was the Bank's most traditional source of income, whose volumes varied with the seasons. Even allowing for this, income rose from around £100,000 in 1772 to £1 million in 1800, with a consequent rise in profits, even when the margins on loans were being squeezed by inflation during the 1790s. The cash credit was theoretically renewable each year, but this tended to be rolled over year on year and increased in line with a particular business's expansion. The evidence is not wholly clear-cut but there are strong indications that in many, perhaps most, businesses the cash credit was used to deal with day-to-day fluctuations in cash flow rather than for capital development. In most partnerships or single-owner firms this appears to have been achieved by reinvestment of profits. On the other hand, direct loans were made for infrastructure projects, for example £8,000 to the City of Edinburgh towards the building of the South Bridge, and £10,000 to the Leith Docks and Harbour development.

The clearest indication of the role the Bank played in Scotland is that it was able, and willing, to grant loans at little or no interest to burghs to buy grain or meal for distribution to the poor in years of bad harvests and high prices. The worst year was 1782, when Edinburgh received £5,000, Ayr £2,000, Aberdeen £3,000, Stirling £1,000, Dumfries £800, and Dunfermline, Kirkcaldy, Inverness, Kelso, Kilmarnock, Banff and Elgin £500 each, all interest free. Similar loans were made in 1795, 1796, 1799 and 1800.

Bank of Scotland's influence was increased by the spread of branches and agencies throughout Scotland. The first five in order of founding – Dumfries and Kelso in 1774 and Kilmarnock, Ayr and Inverness Union Street in 1775 – were all started in areas where the Buccleuch–Dundas influence was strongest.

The first agents – David Staig at Dumfries, David Ferguson at Ayr, Robert Scott at Kelso (he was Buccleuch's ex-chamberlain) and John Mackintosh in Inverness – were prominent local figures in their own right with extensive non-banking interests. Staig, for example, was responsible for the transmission of revenue funds from Dumfries and was involved in

Top: *Letter of agreement to co-operation between Bank of Scotland and the Royal Bank of Scotland, dated 1783*

Above: *Letter from the artist Sir Henry Raeburn requesting a loan of £600 on the security of his Bank of Scotland stock*

Right: *Private Act of Parliament to increase the capital of Bank of Scotland*

Inverness in the early nineteenth century by John Clark

Portable coin scales of c.1780

the purchase of the Dalswinton estate for Patrick Miller. In every case where a branch might be considered, it was essential that the agent be a man of local knowledge and standing. By 1778 the five branches plus Stirling, which was added in 1776, showed a total profit of £5,488. By 1795 some 27 branches had been opened of which only two, Paisley and Greenock, faced severe competition from local banking companies.

It is in the matter of a branch in Glasgow that the co-ordination of policy between the Bank and the Royal Bank can be shown most clearly. The main sources of the Royal's profits in the 1770s were the receipts of Customs and Excise, the Commission for Forfeited Estates, the Army and cross-border money transmission. Many of the new provincial banking companies were provided with cash credits by the Royal, which was both an indication of their standing and a guarantee in times of crisis. In Glasgow and the Clyde ports, 1782-83 was an important watershed. The activities of the French fleet in American waters disrupted the West Indies trade, and the surrender of the British Army under Cornwallis at Yorktown, Virginia, in 1781 (where the regimental bands played *The World Turned Upside Down*) effectively finished the Virginia trade. It appears that all the Glasgow banks, with the possible exception of the Ship Bank, required support and extended credit. To deal with this, the Royal opened an agency in Glasgow in 1783 under David Dale and Robert Scott Moncrieff. David Dale had set up the celebrated New Lanark Mills, which quickly became the largest water-powered spinning-mill in Britain, with 1,500 employees. In 1793 around £400,000 of bills were discounted, rising to £700,000 in 1810. Bank of Scotland did not open a Glasgow branch until 1802, by which time it had become obvious that most of the increase in capital of both banks would be required to underwrite the rapid industrialisation of the West of Scotland. At this stage the major contribution of the two Edinburgh banks was to provide a stable platform from which greater entrepreneurial enterprise could be launched. It was a role valuable in its time and place, but one which became unnecessary – or so it seemed – within a generation.

The very existence of a branch network brought the Bank a new series of problems, for which there were few precedents. In December 1784 agents were informed that 'the frequent robberies . . . make it necessary to have another armed servant on horseback added to the former guard, when remittances are sent from the branches'. A loaded pistol was a normal part of the equipment of any bank clerk accompanying remittances to and from branches. Many of these journeys have an epic quality, particularly in winter or early spring. (See page 102, for example.) Most journeys were made on horseback. Transmission of letters to and

84   from St Andrews, for example, required the messenger from the branch to meet the Edinburgh-Perth courier at Cupar in Fife. The exact timing varied according to the season and the weather on the stretch of the Forth Estuary between Leith or Granton and Burntisland or Kirkcaldy. The development of turnpike roads and stagecoaches improved matters, but at no point before the arrival of railways could timing be guaranteed.

In these circumstances there was little alternative to allowing branches a good deal of autonomy and relying upon the agents' indemnity bonds to limit harmful conflicts of interest. Agents were paid high salaries, but the Bank demanded proper security against losses and issued detailed instructions to branches as to the conduct of business (six pages in 1783; now, in 1995, a five-volume blockbuster). Agents were usually required to meet losses on bills of exchange and cash credits, and it was usual for each to be assisted by an accountant and teller. From 1783 branches were inspected by Head Office every eighteen months. These inspections concentrated on a limited number of objectives: that the cash and notes in hand matched the book balances; that all bills were properly listed; that the agents' private accounts were not mixed with those of the Bank; that the security for cash credits and other loans was up to date; and finally that current accounts were properly listed and the interest recorded. What, at this stage of development, the system could not deal with was systematic and deliberate fraud, where the agent's 'friends' were merely a front for manipulating the branch accounts. A case at Haddington branch, which came to light in 1801–2, taught many hard lessons, and although it increased the Bank's vigilance in such matters it could not eliminate the problem completely.

The third element of the Bank's business, and that of all the Scottish banks, was its relationship with its London correspondents. In general these were London-Scots houses; the two used by Bank of Scotland were Hog & Kinloch and Coutts & Co. The relationship was close enough for Coutts to handle secret business for Dundas. The bulk of the ordinary business of the London agents was handling and discounting bills of exchange which was, for all practical purposes, the normal method of money transmission between Edinburgh and London. During the 1780s the volume of this business quadrupled, in itself an indication of a developing, single, 'British' economy, but it became necessary for Bank of Scotland to create reserves in London. This took two forms: short-term cash deposits and longer-term investment in Government stock. The key to permitting the Scots bank to hold such stock was an unwritten agreement that they would be held to maturity and not traded for short-term profit.

The Falls of Clyde by Jacob More (National Gallery of Scotland).
The water of the Falls was harnessed to provide the motive power for
David Dale's cotton spinning factory at New Lanark,
pictured below by John Clark

86

Above: *Letter from James Fraser to Henry Dundas about the crisis in the West of Scotland, 27 April 1793*

Left: *Letter from Sir William Forbes to Henry Dundas hoping that a naval force will be sent to protect Scotland, and discussing the Bank of England suspension, 4 March 1797*

The net result of this was that Bank of Scotland built up very large reserves in London. The close co-operation of the various parts of the system was tested in 1789 in an incident which cannot be explained in any other way than to say that those involved chanced their arm. Public revenues in Scotland were sent to London jointly by the Royal Bank and Sir William Forbes Bank, which had also since 1749 dealt with the excise money of Scotland. The Royal Bank directors wrote to Dundas suggesting that they be given a monopoly in the matter and that Forbes be dropped. Unknown to both, Thomas Coutts, Bank of Scotland's agent in London, had laid claim to the contract for his own bank in a letter to Prime Minister Pitt. The toing and froing was considerable and it was not until 1796 that the whole matter was settled by dividing the revenue business into four and giving a quarter each to the Royal, the British Linen, Sir William Forbes and Bank of Scotland. This was the first time since 1727 that the 'Old' Bank had handled any Government revenues and it added to the feeling of success as the Bank completed its first century. The man who had for a number of years defended Bank of Scotland's interests in London was felt to be worthy of a present in addition to his normal fees and in 1797 the directors paid £127 for an épergne which was engraved and presented to the lawyer James Mansfield 'for his services'.

After 1791 Henry Dundas, now Home Secretary, was at the peak of his power and influence, but in Scotland itself the Government was unpopular with Whig and radical advocates of reform. The French Revolution of 1789 itself enjoyed considerable support from no less a person than the Earl of Lauderdale as well as from academics and the educated middle classes of Scotland. It is also tempting to conclude that Patrick Miller's offer of a farm near Dumfries to Robert Burns in 1788 and the latter's employment as an exciseman under David Staig was, if not an attempt to bribe Scotland's national poet, at least an encouragement to him to modify the criticism of Scotland's rulers which may be found in some of the poems he wrote between 1790 and 1792.

In 1791 the harvest was bad and, as the expansion of trade began to falter, the Bank began to draw in credit. The outbreak of war with France on 11 February 1793 precipitated a major crisis of confidence: bills were returned unpaid, goods and raw materials were

A late eighteenth-century flintlock pistol, originally from Kelso branch

88 hoarded, manufacturing orders were cancelled and Government stock fell sharply in value. From Bank of Scotland's point of view the problem was a sharp banking dilemma: it needed to realise a substantial part of its London reserves to support both the Royal Bank and its own operations, mostly in Glasgow, but did not want either to break agreements or to sell at the bottom of the market. In addition, a number of the provincial banks needed support from the chartered banks. Sir William Forbes's *Memoir* records the anxieties of the next two months. The scheme devised by the banks and presented to Dundas and Pitt was for the issue of exchequer bills against the security of goods already in warehouses via a small number of approved firms to restart the economy. For Britain as a whole, just over £2 million of exchequer loans were made, of which £404,000 was necessary in Scotland. Of this latter sum £350,000 went to Glasgow and Paisley, while only £54,000 was required for the rest of the country. In this situation it was the Royal Bank which suffered most severely, at one point requiring a loan of £150,000 from Bank of Scotland. The Government's action prevented a commercial crisis becoming a catastrophe, although there were inevitably a number of casualties among manufacturers and some of the lesser banks. On the whole, from the summer of 1793, businesses made a swift recovery, in part because the actual needs of war required continual Government spending.

As the war progressed, mostly on land and in France's favour, problems of disruption to export trade gradually accumulated and added to the strains of the Government's own borrowings of £100 million. One major consideration was the steady drain of gold from the Bank of England, partly sent abroad for payment or trade and partly hoarded at home. The crisis broke on 23 February 1797, when there was a French landing at Fishguard, in Wales. Panic ensued. Gold was withdrawn from circulation and on 26 February the Privy Council issued an order forbidding the Bank of England from issuing any more specie until further notice. The carefully nurtured paper currency system of Scotland was under severe strain. On 1 March the Court of Session passed a resolution supporting the suspension. However, public meetings were held in both Edinburgh and Glasgow to support the banks, which continued to receive each other's bank-notes. The crisis was contained but the real need was for small-denomination currency to replace silver, which had also disappeared. A variety of token coinages appeared for small amounts; and Bank of Scotland and other banks, whose notes were 'as good as gold', issued (contrary to the 1765 Act) a large number of five-shilling bank-notes, which had a very short life as they passed from hand to hand.

In spite of all this, the 1790s saw the fastest rate of growth in the Bank's history: net profits rose from £31,013 in 1791 to £89,200 in 1800, a figure which was sustained through 1801 and 1802. Over the same period, the value of bills on London increased four times, while the income from branches went from £19,580 to £68,215. By 1802 the Bank's business in Glasgow had even overtaken that of the Royal.

At the Bank's general meeting of 1796, on completion of one hundred years of trading, it was with great confidence that the Directors announced that they were to begin looking for a site on which to build a new Head Office. There were a number of considerations and constraints on the search. Firstly, the site had to be within the bounds of the Old Town, in part because property within the main area of Edinburgh's New Town contained covenants restricting usage to domestic occupation, and in part because the core business area of Edinburgh remained around Parliament Square and the Lawnmarket. Secondly, the property was to be free-standing and not approached through a vennel or court. The Bank's customers had ample experience of Edinburgh's method of waste disposal in Gourlay's Close: 'gardyloo' cost many a pair of silk stockings. The problem grew worse as the properties fronting the High Street degenerated into slums. Thirdly, there was an acknowledgment that the new Head Office should adequately reflect the prestige and central role of the Bank.

In 1800 a suitable site became available, the result of the Town Improvement Commissioners' demolition of tenements on the north side of the Lawnmarket from Lady Stair's Close to Dunbar's Close. The approach street had already been named Bank Street and seemed to bridge the gap between the Old and New Towns via the Mound, then known as 'Geordie Boyd's Mud Brig'. The land cost £1,350, and plans for the Bank House on the Mound were prepared by Robert Reid and Richard Crichton, two promising pupils of the architect Robert Adam. The plans were approved by the Dean of Guild in 1802 (hardly surprising since Crichton was Clerk) and excavations began. Because the new building was to be sited on the junction between the basalt rock of Edinburgh High Street and the travelled earth of the Mound (essentially the excavated spoil from New Town foundations), the footings were substantial. Excavations caused slippage of some properties in Bank Street and the collapse of a whole tenement, a matter whose financial implications were still unsettled ten years later. The building, which faced the Old Town and presented its rear to the New Town, was a late Georgian villa of four storeys with a shallow dome and the coat-of-arms of the Bank, carved by John Marshall, above the front door. The financing of

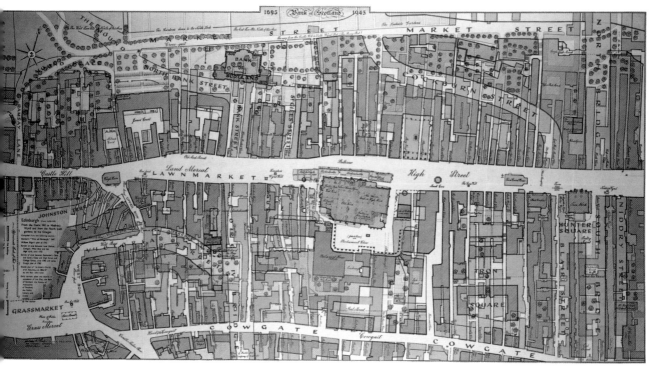

*Plan of Edinburgh Old Town redrawn in 1945 showing the locations of
the Bank Head Office, 1695–1995*

the building is in itself an object lesson, one to which the Proprietors were
never party. In each of the five financial years between 1800 and 1805, £5,000
was withdrawn from the Bank's undivided profits and placed in a separate
account which was reinvested, partly in the Bank's own stock. This had
accumulated to some £30,000 by 1819, when it was decided finally to apply
the sum to the building costs of £43,000. The Bank House was therefore
placed on the Bank's books as being 'worth' £13,000.

In many ways the Bank House provided the model layout for bank
houses erected in most of Scotland's towns during the succeeding century.
There was an impressive entrance which gave access to the telling room
and offices on the ground floor with some Directors' rooms on the first
floor, but above and below the business floors were domestic quarters. The
former were occupied by the Cashier and his family and the latter by the
bank messenger. There was no formal opening of the building, but on 12
August 1806 the staff of the Bank moved papers, ledgers and cash to the
new Bank House and opened for business. The whole process from
decision to occupation took ten years and six months. The architects each
received presents of £150, and a fire insurance policy worth £5,100 for the
building and £100 for the contents was taken out with the Edinburgh
Friendly Insurance Company.

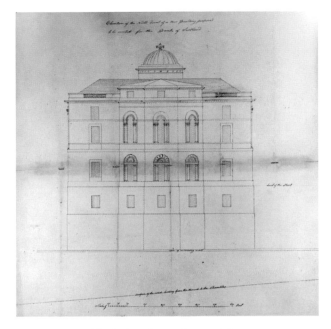

*North elevation and ground floor
plan of proposed Bank House by
Crichton and Reid*

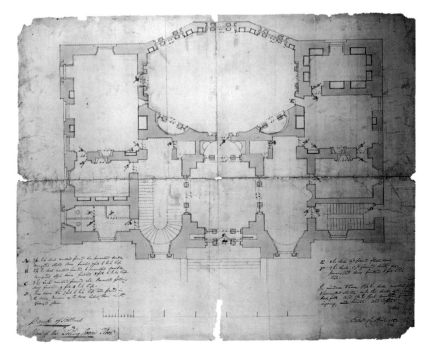

The Bank House on the Mound in 1809

While the Bank had been building, the world had moved on. By 1800, although the British fleet dominated the seas, French armies controlled mainland Europe and there was an effective stalemate. The Pitt–Dundas combination seemed to have failed and in 1801 Henry Addington became Prime Minister. The Treaty of Amiens, which temporarily halted the Anglo-French conflict, was accompanied by retrenchment in public expenditure and a decline in Dundas's control of Scotland. Peace lasted barely two years, and the threat of war in 1803 brought with it bankruptcies and speculation in commodities in Scotland of which, for once, the Bank had ample warning – one of the benefits of a branch network, namely better communications. Despite this, there was a major financial crisis for both the Royal and the Bank because the Government and the Bank of England refused to provide the support which would have produced confidence.

For Bank of Scotland, bad debt provisions rose sharply, and the return to power of Dundas, now first Viscount Melville, was only a temporary respite. His political enemies charged him with corruption, particularly over his handling of the Navy and Scottish revenue accounts. The two Scottish banks were not named but they were implicated in the charges. Although Melville was cleared at a trial before his peers in 1806, the system over which he had presided fell apart and many of Bank of Scotland's agents and contacts were tainted. As if to confirm the end of an old system, in 1806 the British Linen

Company had its authorised capital increased to £200,000, and in 1810 an entirely new co-partnery bank, the Commercial Bank of Scotland, was formed in Edinburgh from among the Whig interest, which included the advocate Henry Cockburn, better known in his later role as the judge Lord Cockburn.

The period after 1806 to the end of the war was profitable for many of the Bank's agricultural and business customers, and this is reflected in both the market price of Bank stock and the dividend paid, which averaged 7½ per cent between 1811 and 1815. At the close of a generation of war in 1815 the Bank was illuminated and the Directors made loans for the extension of Princes Street to the east, the streets known, appropriately enough, as Waterloo Place, Regent Road and Regent Terrace.

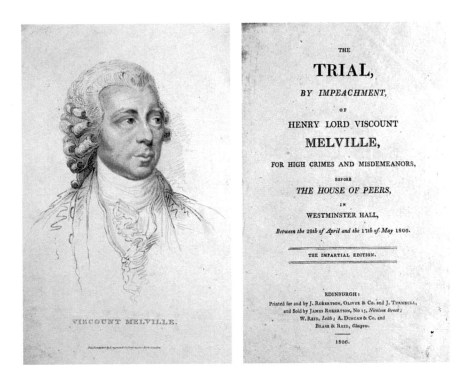

Two pages from a report of the trial of Lord Melville

—Lines Written on a Bank-note—

Wae worth thy power, thou cursed leaf!
Fell source o a' my woe and grief,
For lack o thee I've lost my lass,
For lack o thee I scrimp my glass!
I see the children of affliction
Unaided, through thy curs'd restriction.
I've seen the oppressor's cruel smile
Amid his hapless victims' spoil;
And for thy potence vainly wish'd,
To crush the villain in the dust.
For lack o thee, I leave this much-lov'd shore,
Never, perhaps, to greet old Scotland more.

R.B.
Kyle

This poem was written by Robert Burns on the back of a Bank of Scotland guinea note dated 1 March 1780, and the holograph is among the manuscripts preserved at the Burns Cottage at Alloway. The context of the poem is clear enough. In September 1785 Burns 'attested' his marriage to Jean Armour, but it was only revealed to Jean's father, James, when he discovered his daughter's pregnancy in February 1786. Burns was repudiated as a son-in-law by the Armour family and Jean was sent off to relatives in Paisley. About this time he began to contemplate emigrating to Jamaica but postponed a decision until after the first edition of his poems was published (the first Kilmarnock edition) in April 1786. In the meantime, Burns met Mary Campbell (Highland Mary) and they made plans to emigrate together. In June, Burns appeared before the Kirk Session at Mauchline and in July, still planning to emigrate, went into hiding after Jean Armour got a writ to 'throw me into jail till I find security for an enormous sum'. The poem seems to reflect his financial situation at this time, which was relieved by the success of *Poems, chiefly in the Scottish Dialect*, published on 31 July (at 3s.). Also written, and then included in the second edition, is the poem 'On a Scotch Bard gone to the West Indies'. The voyage to Jamaica was postponed during September, the month that Jean Armour gave birth to their twins, Robert and Jean. In October, emigration was abandoned after the death of Mary Campbell at Greenock, possibly in premature childbirth. It is from this point in time that Robert Burns begins to think of a career as an exciseman.

OPPOSITE PAGE:
Robert Burns in 1787 by Alexander Nasmyth (National Gallery of Scotland)
Holograph lines on a bank-note (Burns Monument, Alloway)

Bank of Scotland
Edinr.
One Guinea
1st March 1780.
The Governor and Compa
of the Bank of Scotland
One Pound One Shilling on de
By order of the Court of Directo
Fell source of all my woe and grief!
I see the children of Affliction
I've seen th' Oppressor's cruel smile
And for thy potence vainly wish'd
To crush the Villain in the dust:
Never perhaps to greet old Scotland more
R. B.

Bank of Scotland one guinea note of 1780

Drawing by Thomas Watling of a white-tailed warbler
(British Museum of Natural History)

—8—

BANK-NOTES AND FORGERY, 1780–1815

FOR a bank which issued its own bank-notes, detecting and stopping forgery was a normal part of the control of note issue before 1770. Forgery was on the whole quite small-scale and did not appear to pose a great threat to the acceptability of paper currency. Detection required alertness and a good 'eye'. In 1767 James Balfour, one of the Bank's accountants, requested permission to employ someone at his own expense temporarily because he had an eye problem which made it difficult for him to do his job, which included maintenance of the note-issue books. The Bank agreed and there was no shortage of applicants. With the development of a branch network in towns such as Dumfries, where Bank of Scotland notes predominated and were treated as part of other banks' reserves, the problem grew. The appearance of a forged note in a particular town did not necessarily mean that it had been manufactured there. In Dumfries during the 1770s and '80s there was a steady trickle of forged notes whose author escaped detection. There is now evidence to suggest that they were made in Belfast and shipped into various west coast ports – notably Dumfries, Ayr and Greenock – since they all appear to be from the same hand.

It was, however, the Bank's one-guinea note, designed in 1780, which attracted most forgery attempts. One of the more unusual concerned the artist Thomas Watling. He was born in Dumfries in 1762 and was a skilled artist and painter who started his own drawing academy. On 27 November 1788 he was arrested in Dumfries and charged with forging at least 12 Bank of Scotland one-guinea notes.

Dumfries, December 2

On Thursday last, after a long examination before the Sheriff Substitute of Dumfries, was committed to the prison of this place, a young man, for being concerned in forgeries on the Bank of Scotland and British Linen Company.

The Sheriff Substitute, in seaching the young man's lodgings, found in a drawer a half-finished guinea note, in imitation of the Bank of Scotland's notes, which left no doubt of his guilt. This young man endeavoured to criminate another person of this town; but the account given being so very contradictory, and totally unsupported by the evidence he condescended on, and the other person's innocence having appeared to the entire satisfaction of all concerned in the investigation, the Sheriff Substitute dismissed him.

Dumfries Weekly Journal, December 1788

Watling was described as a 'young man of unripe years', and although he attempted to implicate a Dumfries engraver, John Roberts, as the principal, he was found guilty and on 14 April 1789 sentenced to transportation for 14 years to the colony founded just a year earlier, Botany Bay. After two years in the prison hulks in Plymouth Harbour he finally reached Port Jackson, Australia, on 7 October 1792, the first professional artist to reach the colony. He was placed in the charge of the surgeon general, John White, and began to record in descriptions and drawings the flora and fauna of the continent. In Penrith in 1794 his *Letters from an Exile to his Aunt in Dumfries* were published and in them he gives a vivid account of the countryside and climate and of the customs of the native inhabitants. Watling seems to have got on well with the aborigines, and his extensive collection of paintings and drawings is the main visual record of the earliest decade of British settlement in Australia.

> Sydney Cove, from where I write . . . is the principal settlement, and is about one third part as large as Dumfries. . . . When you write to me, be so kind as to inform me of every little incident in Dumfries. Your new bridge and theatre I have already heard of . . .

In 1796 Watling was conditionally pardoned and on 5 April 1797 this was made absolute and he left Australia. He returned home via India and by 1803 was back in Dumfries, where he became art master at the academy at a salary of six guineas a year. Clearly this was not enough and he was tempted into making new bank-note plates. In 1805 he was arrested and again charged with the forgery of seven Bank of Scotland £5 notes. Three were passed by him, and both the teller and David Staig, the agent, gave evidence against him. The jury found the charge not proven, however, and he was freed. His later years were penurious and he appears to have died of cancer in 1814–15.

Between 1811 and 1814 a series of forgeries of £1 and one-guinea notes was discovered, not only those of Bank of Scotland but of the other banks as well. These were eventually traced back to French prisoners-of-war held in Edinburgh Castle and in the camps at Penicuik, the largest complex of its kind in Scotland and second only to the cage at Norman Cross in Northamptonshire. The forgery was a large-scale effort requiring the active co-operation of outsiders. It is more than likely that forgeries were commissioned by the guards in return for small favours or improvements to the conditions, which for most prisoners were decidedly spartan. At first the majority of prisoners were seamen, but by 1810 a large number of soldiers began to appear as a result of Wellington's successes in Spain and Portugal. For officers who were prepared to be paroled and live quietly in the neighbourhood, life could be pleasant, if dull. The British Linen Company's agent in Cupar was responsible for handling the parole of officers in central Fife. The parole book (see illustration) records the physical appearance of each prisoner, whose description would have been circulated had there been any attempt to break parole and escape. For the majority of ordinary prisoners, camp life was monotonous and at times distinctly harsh. It is estimated that in the three camps around Penicuik between 1803 and 1814 there were some 11,000 prisoners; and although described as 'French', they included many nationalities, particularly Danes and Swedes among the seamen. As so often happens, the gap between the rations officially supplied by the War Department and what the prisoners actually ate was a large one. Food was always meagre and scarce and, as in many similar circumstances, the guards encouraged trading and private enterprise. Activity was a necessary antidote to despair and lassitude, and on 25 September 1811 the Edinburgh *Evening Courant* reported that three prisoners from Greenlaw camp in Penicuik were in the Tolbooth, the city's main prison, on suspicion of forgery. The outcome of this incident is not known, but combating forgery became a regular feature of the Bank's concerns over the next three years. The Bank published advertisements offering a reward of £100 to anyone who could provide information leading to the conviction of the perpetrators within three months. The forged notes were normally made by hand with pen and pencil, without any engraving. 'In most of them the body of the notes has the appearance of foreign handwriting. The names of the bank officers, though common and well known in this

*Parole book for French prisoners-of-war 1808-15, maintained by
the agent of the British Linen Company in Cupar, Fife*
Below: *Description of the elements of forgery which would
permit their detection*

country, are in the forged notes most illegible or wrong spelled.' In fact 101
they were easy to detect because of a variety of imperfections, but that
they appeared in circulation at all was worrying to the Bank. A steady
trickle of prisoners were detected as forgers and a number were sent to
the hulks at Chatham, Portsmouth or Plymouth, but none was ever
formally tried and convicted. In retrospect perhaps this was fair enough
since the real culprits were the members of the Aberdeen or
Kirkcudbrightshire militia who guarded them and 'the riff raff of
Edinburgh who came to see the prisoners and to profit by their illicit
activity'. One case which was defended by Lord Cockburn concerned
Thomas Gray, a soldier in the Kirkcudbrightshire militia, who was found
to be in possession of £33 of forged notes. Gray was sentenced to 14
years' transportation in 1814 but this was reduced almost immediately
by the Prince Regent to six months' imprisonment. Others were not so
lucky. Nathaniel Blair was sentenced to death, and cheated the
executioner only by hanging himself in his own cell.

The most surprising souvenir of these events which the Bank
possesses is a set of mutton and rabbit bones carved by hand to provide
instruments of forgery. Some at least seem a little unlikely since if ever
used they would have reproduced the Bank of Scotland's name as mirror
writing!

Bones carved by French prisoners-of-war in the camp at Glencorse,
Penicuik, for forging Bank of Scotland notes

—The Pursuit of Forgers from— Dumfries

It was rare for the Bank's clerks to have an opportunity of chasing and capturing forgers of the Bank's notes. Yet there were two occasions in 1779 – in September and October – when the staff at the Dumfries branch had to prepare for the capture of two separate gangs. On September 5 James Graham and William Macdowall, pistols primed, took seats in a post-chaise and set out to arrest three men – David and William Reid and William McWhirr, whose physical appearance was known and who were implicated in the forgery of the Bank's pound notes. After many days' travel the clerks were successful, two of the culprits being caught in Stranraer, the third in Portpatrick.

—ACCOUNT—
of expences laid out in detecting DAVID REID'S forgery upon the Bank of Scotland

Mr James Graham and William Macdowall left Dumfries in pursuit of the forgers the 8th day of September 1779 and apprehended Willm Reid and Willm McWhirr at Stranraer, and David Reid at Portpatrick, whom they lodged in Dumfries-prison after 5 days absence.

THEIR EXPENCES

Hire of two horses 83 miles @ 3d. p. mile	£2	1	6
ditto of two chaises back to Dumfries with the 3 prisoners 83 ms. @ 11d.	7	12	2
ditto of a chaise from Stranraer to Portpatrick after David Reid		7	0
ditto of a saddle horse for one of the Soldiers doun to Dumfries		18	-
paid two chaise drivers for 7 stages each	1	-	6
paid hostlers for chaises and saddle horses going and coming		12	9
Maintenance of ourselves and horses going up when we called at every alehouse upon the road to make enquiry	3	12	11
Bill at Taylor's Stranraer for ourselves and some friends who sat up all night with us taking the precognition	1	1	4
ditto at Alexander's Stranraer for the Prisoners and Military and charge for confusing and taking up the house on the fair day	1	16	10
ditto at Portpatrick for constable and military		5	-
Maintenance of ourselves, the prisoners, military, constable and saddle horses from Stranraer to Dumfries-prison	4	17	7
Paid two men as Scouts at the fair of Stranraer		7	6
Paid Serjeant and party for guarding the prisoners part of two days and a night at Stranraer, there being no prison	1	7	-

Paid Corporal two soldiers and Constable for attending the prisoners to Dumfries	4	5	-
Paid Jail-ffees etc. at imprisoning the prisoners in Dumfries		7	8
Paid Express from Stranraer to Provost Fergusson at Ayr		8	-
Paid Sundry Incidents particulars for which are forgot	1	3	10

Mr Graham and W. Macdowall set out for Kendal fells 15 September 1779 to search for the plates hid there by David Reid, they travelling at night and the weather being rainy took chaise and were absent five days.

THEIR EXPENCES

Hire of a chaise for 182 miles @ 11d. p. mile – having gone twice from Penrith to the 11th mile stone beyond Shap	8	6	10
Chaise-drivers being rainy and often under night	1	5	-
Paid Tollbars, Waiters, Hostlers and Chambermaids		19	2
Paid labourers for digging near two days for the plates		8	-
Maintenance going and coming and at rendering account to the Sheriff of our proceedings	3	11	-

Mr Graham and William Macdowall set out for Mochrum in the shire of Galloway to have John Stewart apprehended on suspicion of his being either an accomplice of or useful witness agt. D. Reid, and were absent three days.

THEIR EXPENCES

Hire of two horses to Newton Stewart 48 miles @ 3d. p. mile	1	4	-
ditto of a chaise from ditto to Mochrum		17	-
Hire of a horse for Stewart to ride to Dumfries upon		10	6
paid a Constable for going from Wigtown to apprehend Stewart		6	6
Maintenance of ourselves, Stewart and 3 horses till our return to Dumfries including waiters &ca.	2	18	3
paid Stewart's expences being 8 days detailed in Dumfries till instructions came from Edinburgh and his bail bond was executed	1	19	11
paid expences of his horse for same time		9	4
paid express to Wigtown with Stewart's bail bond for execution		15	-
paid Constable for 5 days attending Stewart in Dumfries		7	6
paid Sheriff's Officer for ditto		4	6
paid Stewart in order to carry him home		10	-

22 November 1779 William Macdowall set out upon a journey through the different places the forgers had been in order to take precognitions and discover who would be useful evidence upon David Reid's trial, which took 13 days in March 1780. The whole cost to the Bank of pursuing the forgers and a successful prosecution totalled £128 17s. 11d.

To the Treasurer   Bank of Scotland 29 Sept 1815

You will pay the Company's Servants one quarter's Salary ended this day as under   James Marshall Accountant

Name	Office	£ p. ann.	Copy Tax	1st Quarter
Robert Forrester	Treasurer	400	10 .	100 .
George Sandy	Secretary	220	5 10	55
James Marshall	Accountant	270	6 15	67 10
Robert Coventry	Teller	236	5 18	59
Henry Goodsir	Do	218	5 9	54 10
Walter Thomson	Do	190	4 15	47 10
Patrick Michlejohn	Do	172	4 6	43 .
William Forrester	Do	167	4 3 6	41 15
George Paterson asst Do		90	1 10	22 10
James Frazer, Clerk in Accts office		160	4 .	40 .
William Bachim	Do	170	4 5	42 10
John Slim	Do	210	5 5	52 10
John Hogg	Do	175	4 7 6	43 15
James Hutchison	Do	120	2 12 6	30
Andrew Young	Do	105	2 1 5	26 5
Joseph Radcliff	Do	90	1 10 .	22 10
Alex Russell	Do	90	1 10 .	22 10
Gilbert Hutchison	Do	50		12 10
Archibald Bennet Secretaries office		200	5 .	50 .
Patrick Maxton	Do	140	3 2 6	35 .
Will Buchan Junr	Do	75	1 8 9	18 15
Patrick Bennet	Do	50		12 10
Andrew Sime Printer		85		21 5
Angus McDonald, Geo Wilson & John Mackie	each	50		37 10
Donald Fisher Porter	18/ p week	82 19 1		11 14

Salary sheet for Head Office staff for the quarter ending 29 September 1815.
The Treasurer, Robert Forrester, had £400 a year, and the Secretary £220 a year.

—9—

DOLDRUMS AND UNCERTAINTY, 1815–55

T HE two decades after the Battle of Waterloo saw a reversal of the Bank's fortunes and the slide into a trough from which it took nearly a generation to recover. Although after the death in 1812 of Henry Dundas, first Viscount Melville, the governorship was offered to and accepted by his son, the second Viscount, the Bank was no longer able to rely on political management to protect its interests. The low point was 1831–32, and recovery was only achieved by the application of strict banking principles. Part of the problem, which was not unique to Bank of Scotland, was that the second phase of industrialisation in Scotland produced a much more demanding and complex banking environment. This in its turn required a substantial shift in policy-making within the Bank from the Board of amateur (if enthusiastic) Directors to professional managers. One consequence of the Bank's difficulties was that in the 1830s and 1840s it was in no position to take full advantage of the opportunities generated in the West of Scotland. It also had to face the full impact of competition provided by the new Glasgow-based joint-stock banks, most notably the Glasgow Union Bank (later the Union Bank of Scotland) in 1830 and the Western Bank in 1832. By 1850 the paid-up capital of these new banks together amounted to some £5,663,700 as against £3,500,000 for the original three public banks in Edinburgh. In rank order, Bank of Scotland declined from first position to sixth in terms of liabilities and deposits and to fifth in terms of advances. It is ironic that this should have been the underlying reality of Bank of Scotland's situation precisely when it was enjoying its greatest reputation furth of Scotland.

106   In 1815 demand for the war effort had been the source of prosperity for many of the Bank's customers in the iron-founding and textile industries. Peace reduced opportunities for firms like the Carron Iron Company, whose chief product, light cannon, was no longer in demand. The expansion of such companies had been achieved during a period of inflation, when borrowing was relatively cheap, a situation which changed as prices stabilised and then fell during the 1820s. It was the Bank's farming constituency which had to make the greatest adjustments. During the Napoleonic Wars, Britain's farmers had a virtual monopoly over agricultural products in the home market. By 1814 the boom in agriculture which had been the reason for 'improvement' on many estates was over, and the price of oats, barley and wheat fell steadily, discouraging new investment. Some of the changes were permanent. Much of the land in Buchan and the north-east had been won for agriculture, planted for the first time, and the landscape of fermtouns with its bothies created from scratch. But on West Highland estates the fall in the price of cattle and kelp produced a financial crisis for many landowners. For example, between 1799 and 1811 the rental income from Lord Macdonald's estate on Skye rose from £5,500 to £14,000. Attempts to maintain these income levels between 1815 and 1830 meant that new sources of income were needed and he began the process of replacing people with sheep in the clearances on his Skye and Uist estates. The price of kelp had risen from two or three pounds a ton in the 1780s to £20 a ton just after the turn of the century as a result of the war with France. Then the kelp-burning industry collapsed quickly after the removal of duties on Norwegian kelp in 1813. The price of the alkali created by kelp-burning fell by two-thirds between 1817 and 1827, despite the fact that it was of prime importance in the soap and glass industries, both of which were expanding. Applications for loans from Mackenzie of Seaforth, the principal landowner on the Isle of Lewis, appear in the Bank records in the 1820s, couched in terms of greatest optimism about the benefits of 'development' on his property. In all cases these were rejected because the extended cash credits simply added to the indebtedness of the estate, which Mackenzie was already having difficulty in servicing.

The route to survival often involved leasing out part or all of the estate to successful industrialists or southerners, while attempts were made to rebuild family fortunes in public service or commerce in the colonies. This was the route chosen by the Grants of Rothiemurchus and the Macleods of Dunvegan. Others, like Archibald McNab of McNab, spent years trying to keep one step ahead of the bailiffs; when that failed in 1822 he attempted to relaunch his fortunes by a fraudulent settlement scheme at the junction of the Ottawa and Madawaska Rivers in Upper Canada (modern Ontario Province).

Between 1813 and 1820 the Bank's net income from its branches, mostly in rural areas, fell sharply from £61,363 to a mere £859. As a result, the branches in Tain, Huntly, Montrose and Wigtown were closed, while the branch in Greenock was closed because it was losing business to the Greenock Banking Company. The Edinburgh private banks, which provided a number of Bank Directors, were particularly badly affected by these changes, since all were heavily involved in agricultural lending and, as a result, during the 1820s they stopped being a major part of the general banking scene. The East Lothian Bank, which had been founded on the premise of agricultural prosperity and engaged in speculation in wheat and barley prices (what would now be called trading in agricultural futures), went bankrupt in 1822. The private banks were forced to sell their shareholdings in the Bank and to reduce the quantity of Bank of Scotland bank-notes held as part of their reserves. The situation was such that even Sir John Sinclair of Ulbster, the foremost advocate of agricultural improvement, was forced to sell most of his Bank shares to pay off his overdraft.

The Bank had two methods of dealing with this situation. The first and most obvious was gradually to contract its agricultural lending and switch it into more profitable areas, particularly new industries or companies, which were by definition more risky investments. The second, seen as vital by the Directors in view of the sales of Bank stock, was to ensure that there was no crisis of confidence among the Bank's Proprietors. Stock was bought in and released gradually to flatten out short-term fluctuations in the price and to discourage speculation. (This is now illegal in the UK.) It was also seen as important to maintain the dividend paid out to Proprietors so that the shares continued to trade at a premium. After the immediate post-war slump in 1815–17, business began to pick up. In 1818, buoyed up by the windfall profits made on handling coin for the reminting of the United Kingdom coinage in 1816–17, a special bonus of £200,000 was paid out of reserves over and above the £95,000 declared as the 'normal' dividend, a total return on each share of 29.5 per cent. Between 1819 and 1824 the normal dividend was maintained at 9.5 per cent. From 1824 it was reduced to 8 per cent and then in 1827 to 6 per cent. The dividend reduction in the financial year 1824/25 was softened by a further special bonus of £200,000 which was taken from reserves. These bonuses were crucial to maintaining the share price, particularly in 1818 when £31,784 had to be provided for bad and doubtful debts, as against a previous ten-year average of around £1,800. Between 1810 and 1814 the

Paisley in the 1820s by John Clark

price of £100 of Bank stock had stayed at around £170. In 1817 it stood, before the bonus, at £174. The price leapt to £254 in 1818 and stayed above £235 until 1824. It looked as though the price would fall, but the second bonus pushed the stock to an all-time high of £276 in February 1825, after which it fell away steadily to stand at £198 in 1831 and continued to slide during the 1830s until January 1841, when it sold at £162, the same price as in 1809.

In 1824 the policies with which the Directors charged William Cadell of Tranent when they appointed him Treasurer, with additional powers as General Manager, were as follows:

(1) to enlarge the branch network wherever an opportunity presented;
(2) to look for new investment opportunities;
(3) in co-operation with the other banks, to attempt to control or reduce the price paid for deposits; and
(4) to use the reserves in difficult times to maintain the dividend to Proprietors to counteract speculation in Bank stock.

William Cadell faced a major national crisis within a year of taking office. By the summer of 1825 there was high confidence in the national economy. A boom was fuelled by the repeal of the South Sea Bubble Act of 1720, which had contained specific restrictions on speculative share dealing. There were many new company formations, particularly in ventures associated with the cotton trade and those involved with newly independent states in South

St Andrews in the 1820s by John Clark

America. The problems had become obvious by the late summer. In Scotland, particularly in Paisley and the west, speculators used funds, including bank loans, to hold large stocks of cotton in warehouses, raising the price to the mill owners. Spinners wanted higher wages, and many mills went onto half-time working. The net result was that the Bank of England, fearing a balance of trade deficit and the loss of gold overseas, contracted credit and precipitated a full-scale monetary crisis. Sixty banks failed in England, compared with only three in Scotland – the Stirling Banking Company, the Falkirk Banking Company and the Fife Banking Company – which retired or failed in the subsequent five years. The crisis did not have the same devastating impact north of the Border as it had in England. Although it was regretted in London that the Royal, the British Linen Company and Bank of Scotland did not have confidential understandings, the three agreed to raise interest rates to prevent the outflow of funds. All the five major Scottish banks (the Bank, the Royal, the British Linen, the Commercial and the newly founded National) provided funds to hard-pressed customers and extended overdrafts to customers and other banks. There was no panic in Scotland, because paper currency had been around for so long that there was little temptation to demand specie in exchange.

The most famous casualty of these events was Sir Walter Scott, author and impresario of George IV's visit to Edinburgh in 1822, an event which the Bank celebrated with fireworks and by illuminating the Bank House on

110   the Mound. Sir Walter was a partner in Ballantyne & Company, which became involved in the bankruptcy of the firm of Constable & Company, and was relying on this plus the income from his novels and from investments to underwrite the costs of building his house, Abbotsford. In 1818 Bank of Scotland had granted a cash credit of £1,000 to James Ballantyne and Company towards the purchase price of £1,850 for the *Edinburgh Weekly Journal*. It was assumed, although it was not then revealed, that Scott was a partner in the company. Another member was Robert Cadell, brother of the Bank's Treasurer, William Cadell. When the latter's stewardship of the Bank's affairs came under scrutiny in 1830, he was fiercely criticised for having allowed his brother to clear his deposit account the day before the collapse. At the time of the collapse of Constable & Company Sir Walter's debts amounted to £104,082, of which £40,000 consisted of short-term bills payable on London. There were additional publishers' debts, for which the author felt morally bound if not strictly liable. Sir Walter's largest creditors were Sir William Forbes and Bank of Scotland, although his day-to-day accounts were held at the British Linen Company branch, first in Jedburgh and then in Selkirk. The second Sir William Forbes was the prime mover in putting together the rescue package for Scott in January 1826. The London bill brokers who would not agree were bought off. Abbotsford and all Sir Walter's debts were placed in a trust guaranteed for his lifetime but into which all his earnings would be paid. So faithful was he to his friends that his efforts almost certainly hastened his death. It is a matter of record that Scott's debtors had received 13s. in the £1 by 1832 and that full repayment was completed with Lockhart's edition of his works in 1837–38. It is small wonder that at a public meeting to raise subscriptions for a memorial in Scott's honour it was minuted that:

> The sum of £500 should be subscribed by the Bank of Scotland, the Royal Bank, Sir William Forbes and Company, the British Linen Company, the Commercial Bank, the National Bank and Ramsays, Bonar and Company in token of their admiration of those honourable feelings which induced the late Sir Walter Scott at the time of his embarrassment in 1826 to dedicate his life to insuring [*sic*] full payment to his creditors . . .

To members of Parliament and the public at large the causes of the crash of 1825 seemed clear enough: small-denomination bank-notes and English country banks. An Act was passed which prohibited the issue of bank-notes under £5 in value in England and Wales. Lord Liverpool's Government, perhaps following the advice of Adam Smith fifty years earlier, proposed in February 1826 to extend the Act to Scotland, ironically

Above: *Sir William Forbes of Pitsligo Bt by Sir Henry Raeburn. Forbes was Scott's school and university companion. Their friendship cooled only temporarily in 1797 when they competed for the hand of Elizabeth Belches of Fettercairn. Scott lost.*
Right: *Sir Walter Scott drawing, as prepared for the 1971 series Bank of Scotland notes*
Below: *Cheque signed by Sir Walter Scott drawn on the British Linen Company branch in Selkirk*

The last of the old-style printed bank-notes
for £5 dated 4 March 1824

The first of the Lizar steel-engraved bank-notes.
This technique permitted much finer and more exact
designs to be used to challenge the forger

a move approved of by Lord Melville, the Bank's Governor. This was in spite of the fact that Scots banks seemed to have escaped unscathed; and although it appeared to be little short of a miracle, there were plenty who thought it a conjuring trick. When the proposal became known, Parliament was deluged by petitions from Scotland, from all sectors and interests in society. The arguments were encapsulated in *The Letters of Malachi Malagrowther*, a thinly disguised but well-argued polemic from the pen of Sir Walter Scott, which appeared in March 1826. A Parliamentary Committee sat from March to May of that year taking evidence from Scots bankers on the efficacy of the £1 note. They were virtually unanimous in supporting the Scottish system of banking. For English members the problem became not how to 'tame' the Scottish system, but how to prevent its spread to England, where it would have challenged the Bank of England's monopoly and taken over most of the provincial banking companies. In the end an Act was passed prohibiting the issue of Scottish notes under £5 in England after 5 April 1829.

William Cadell's policy of expansion began to come into effect during 1825 and 1826. Branches were opened or reopened at Fort William, Leith, Stonehaven and Falkirk. New lending to new industries began to appear on the Bank's books, but lending to untried prospects led inevitably to a large and growing bad debt provision. There was also an overhang of irretrievable debts and past-due bills from the 1825-26 crisis which were not provided for. In 1829 two Directors reckoned that in total these stood at £193,293. Many famous names of Scottish industry appear as borrowers at this time, including cotton firms such as Locke and Dunlop, Bogle, and Haddens of Aberdeen, and shipping companies such as the Clydesdale Steam Boat Company. In 1828 the chemical manufacturers Charles Tennant and Company of St Rollox in Glasgow were granted a cash credit of £10,000, which was increased to £40,000 within a decade and at various times reached £100,000. The sheer complexity of the new businesses, for example in distilling, is well illustrated by the relationship between William Haig and the Bank's branch in St Andrews. William Haig was the son-in-law of John Stein, whose family had brought the continuous still to Scotland and which had set up distilleries at Leith and Alloa. William Haig's distillery was established at Guardbridge in Fife at the high point of the tidal estuary of the River Eden. His two farms, Seggie and Monksholm, initially supplied the grain, but as the business grew, more grain had to be imported. The records make it quite clear that the bulk of the grain distillate (hardly whisky) was shipped by sea to London, where it was rectified into 'London' gin. The returning ships picked up grain from East

114 Anglia and coal from Tyneside. To keep up a continuous production, grain had to be stored between harvests. As a sideline, a tile drain and pantile manufactury was set up, whose products are to be found in many fields and on many houses in East Fife to this day. The financial complexities of such a business, dependent on the London market, were considerable. The gap in time between purchase of raw materials and payment for the product could be a year or more. The Bank's role was to finance the stocks and the trade. By 1833 this one account represented 45 per cent of the total lending of St Andrews branch. The local shipowner, John Patterson, who was the carrier, was also on the Bank's books. It gradually became clear that Haig had over-reached himself, and in 1835 over-production and the defalcations of his London agent brought a crisis. The result was a leaseback arrangement of the works to Haig. The Bank took over direct management of the farms of Seggie and Monksholm and brought the account into Head Office. For a generation thereafter, the profits of these two farms appear in the Bank's annual balance. In due course the distillery was taken over by William's son John, who continued until the 1860s. Eventually the site was sold and became the basis of the Guardbridge paper works.

It is easy to overlook the fact that the Bank's business in any town depended crucially upon the character and abilities of the agent. One outcome of the duel in Kirkcaldy (described on page 124) was that the Bank's business among the town's linen manufacturers faded away. When Walter Fergus, a linen manufacturer and shareholder in the Glasgow Union Bank, decided to open a Union Bank branch in 1834, he took most of these accounts out of Bank of Scotland. Even Head Office acknowledged that little could be done until the agent, David Morgan, was gone and that new accounts would depend on new industries. It was the growth of the jute trade, the harbour development and the invention of the linoleum manufacturing process in the 1840s and '50s that gave the Kirkcaldy branch a second lease of life.

A more general and perhaps surprising problem was that despite loans and investments the Bank was actually taking in deposits faster than it could arrange for these to be employed profitably. All the Scottish banks paid interest on deposits, and it required agreement among the Edinburgh banks before the rate could be lowered. In May 1827 it was reduced from 4 to 3 per cent, in May 1828 to 2.5 per cent, and a year later to 2 per cent for sums above £500. It became increasingly clear in the late 1820s, and was commented upon by a number of the Directors, that the accounting systems then in existence did not give a true reflection of the

Bank's position. Between 1827 and 1831 the Bank made an apparent profit of £65,000, enough to cover the 6 per cent dividend paid to shareholders, but this masked inadequate provision for losses and the run-down of the Bank's reserves. When a Directors' Committee began to examine the problems in detail in the summer of 1829 they reached the startling conclusion that virtually *no* profits were made between 1824 and 1829 and that average yearly provision for bad and doubtful debts should have been set at about £50,000. None of this became public knowledge and Cadell was given time to try to change the Bank's course. During 1830 matters got worse, partly but not wholly as a result of uncertainties surrounding the change of regime in France. It was only the threat by a number of the Directors to 'go public' that persuaded the Governor, Lord Melville, both of the seriousness of the situation and that action was required. Negotiations were begun with the Bank of England for a credit of £200,000 on the security of £50,000 of Bank of England shares and £200,000 of 3.5 per cent Government New Annuities.

At the Annual General Meeting in March 1831 the Bank revealed the worst set of trading figures for over a century. There was loud criticism of the management of the Bank, as £30,000 of bad debts had been written off. Resolutions of the meeting included a proposal, which was passed, that the stock qualification for Directors be doubled and that no one who had been a Director within the previous five years was to be eligible for a Bank appointment. In 1832 Lord Melville again reported heavy losses and in July of that year William Cadell resigned. The anger felt at his stewardship of the Bank is illustrated by the fact that consideration of a pension was delayed for a whole year and its payment was nearly blocked by the Annual General Meeting of 1833.

These events severely damaged the reputation of Scots bankers in London, particularly among English politicians. They also demonstrated clearly that the days of amateur, part-time direction of a complex organisation such as a bank were past. Professional skills were needed and every aspect of the Bank's internal control systems and management needed to be overhauled. One of the more important resolutions of the General Meeting was that private bankers should no longer be eligible for election as Directors. There was a strong suspicion – unproven – that such Directors used their position to influence lending policies and provide opportunities for their own banks. In brief, in 1832–33 the last vestiges of Henry Dundas's system of control by the Directors was laid to rest.

From July 1832 the full management of the Bank was given to the newly appointed Treasurer and General Manager, Alexander Blair, who quickly

The Bank House on the Mound from (the present-day) Mound Place, 1830

118   identified two able lieutenants, Charles Campbell, the Bank's agent in
Glasgow, and Archibald Bennet, the Bank Secretary. Under Blair's
direction this trio dominated the Bank's affairs down to the late 1850s. The
Bank was exceptionally fortunate in its choice of Treasurer. Alexander
Blair was a classics scholar who read both Greek and Hebrew; and he was
a close friend of Thomas Tooke, the celebrated contemporary banking
theorist. He began his career with the British Linen Company, first as
confidential clerk, then as assistant secretary and secretary, until in 1828 he
was appointed joint manager with Thomas Corrie. By the time he was
appointed to Bank of Scotland he had already developed a coherent view
of sound banking principles which he could apply to the situation he
found. His first innovation was to collect – in a monthly return of deposits,
loans, cash credits, outstanding bills, note circulation and bad debts – the
detailed information necessary for hands-on control of the Bank. This
permitted adjustments to be made quite quickly and allowed an accurate
overview of the Bank's trading position to be given to the Directors every
six months. It also enabled him to estimate how much of and where the
Bank's reserves and investments could be redeployed. It also allowed the
Bank, for the first time, to calculate the relationship between profits and
share dividend. Charles Campbell was appointed the first Superintendent
of Branches, responsible not only for the audit of their books but also for
assessing the quality of the Bank's business in any town: its viability and
prospects, accounts which might cause or were causing problems, the
competition, and the efficiency or otherwise of any particular agent and
his staff. Campbell's detailed reports form the first entry in a new series of
record books, known as procedure books, one for each branch. These
were maintained in the Superintendent's office and were log books of
recommendations or instructions about the conduct of business.
Archibald Bennet, who had hoped to be made Treasurer, seems to have
accepted the situation and concentrated on the day-to-day management of
Head Office and all legal matters. It was Bennet who introduced the
practice of retaining a law firm to act as the Bank's long-term legal advisers,
one in Glasgow and one in Edinburgh.

During the 1830s a new round of branches opened: Duns in 1832;
Dundee and Lauder in 1833; Fraserburgh, Greenock and Montrose in
1835; Ardrossan and Paisley in 1836; Banchory, Cumnock, Kilmarnock,
Strathaven and Whithorn in 1838; and finally Blairgowrie, Castle Douglas
and Callander between 1839 and 1842, giving the Bank a total of 31
branches by 1845. The strategy of branch opening was dictated by a need
to increase the Bank's lending business in new areas, ahead of the Glasgow

banks. Both the Western Bank, founded in 1832, and the City of Glasgow Bank, founded in 1839, were particularly active in branch formation. For Scotland as a whole, the 1830s was a period of recession, and the additional competition meant that the Bank's profitability continued to decline. During 1840 Alexander Blair conducted an extensive review of the Bank's operations to explain to Directors and dissatisfied Proprietors why, in spite of a great increase in total business, the profits struggled to cover a 6 per cent dividend. Blair argued that there were four reasons for this:

(1) the extensive growth of joint-stock banking: in the 15 years from 1825, 16 new banks had been formed, nine of them between 1838 and 1840. The most important were Glasgow-based, operated on smaller reserves, offered higher rates on deposits and tended to invest in riskier ventures. For the old banks this meant a narrowing of the margin between interest rates on deposits and the yield on Government investments, where most reserves were placed;

(2) the traditional sources of Bank profits, bank-note issuing commissions, and Government revenue handling had all declined in value;

(3) attempts to establish agreed interest rates with other banks and a system of bank charges on customer accounts had failed; and

(4) the creation of branch offices often led to short-term losses.

Western Bank of Scotland specimen £1 note

120   What Alexander Blair did *not* say on this occasion was that his own conservative attitudes to banking, honed by the events of 1830–32, led him to believe that a proven profit of £65,000 should be earned before a 6 per cent dividend was paid and that as a matter of course banks should carry between 25 and 30 per cent of the sum of note issue and deposits as negotiable securities. With these parameters established, Blair could consider diversification of the Bank's investment portfolio and this was precisely the story of the 1840s.

The 1841 Parliament, in the aftermath of a number of English bank failures in 1839, appointed a Select Committee on Banks of Issue; and Blair, as the foremost advocate of classical Scottish banking principles, was invited to give evidence. Once again the suspected culprit was bank-note issue. The immediate motivating force was that the Bank of England's charter was due for renewal in 1844 and Sir Robert Peel, the Home Secretary, saw this as an opportunity for limiting the ability of banks in England and Wales to issue bank-notes. The Committee of Scottish Bank Managers (at first an informal organisation whose existence was not acknowledged publicly) commissioned Blair to deal with the Government, and then orchestrated a stream of protest and petition to prevent the extension of the 1844 Act to Scotland. A compromise was reached in the 1845 Banking Acts, which permitted each bank which issued bank-notes to continue to do so freely up to its average circulation for 1844. Thereafter, if a bank wished to exceed this authorised issue, the excess was to be backed pound for pound in gold and silver in no more than two offices of the bank. For most of the major Scottish banks this meant their Edinburgh and Glasgow offices. No new banks of issue were to be permitted. One important concession made to the Scots was that if two banks merged, their note issue should be combined, rather than – as with English bank mergers – that the note issue should lapse. In fact, the three Edinburgh chartered banks were displeased that no distinction was made between them (in view of their 'tried prudence, usefulness and high respectability and the confidence of the country placed in them') and the joint-stock banks, whose shareholders did not have limited liability. This was special pleading which the Government ignored. The average bank-note circulation at 1844 of the 19 Scottish banks was £3,087,209, of which Bank of Scotland's share was £300,485. By 1865 the Bank was issuing £553,160 in bank-notes, which had risen to £1,079,044 by 1896. Despite the fuss, the blunt fact of the matter is that by 1844 bank-notes were a less important liability for the Bank than deposits. This change in emphasis had occurred within fifty years: in 1802 notes equalled approximately half of total deposits and in 1825 a quarter, but by 1850 the ratio was nearly 1 to 10.

One immediate result of the 1845 Bank Act was that Bank of Scotland had to buy £50,000 of gold from the Bank of England to bring its reserve up to the required balance. In exchange, the Bank of England agreed to receive the transmission of the Bank's remittances of the Scottish Revenue without fee.

The years 1842 to 1844 were years of good harvests and prosperity for the Bank's agricultural customers. This, with the careful watch kept on branches since 1833, had returned the whole system to profit, with only two branches – Kilmarnock and Castle Douglas – showing a small loss. The most volatile business was experienced by the Bank's branches in Airdrie and Paisley which, along with Glasgow, were the only ones in which the amount lent was larger than the sums of money deposited. The Bank's Glasgow business was in the hands of a distinguished series of managers: Charles Campbell was succeeded in 1833 by W.J. Duncan, who resigned from the Bank in 1843 on his appointment as general manager of the National Bank of Scotland; his successor was Andrew Neilson, the fourth generation of his family to serve the Bank. At that time the Bank's office in Glasgow was in cramped premises in Ingram Street at the easternmost end of the city's new business district.

The years 1845 and 1846 were peak times of railway promotion and building. The Bank made numerous loans to Scottish railway companies and authorised its Glasgow manager to lend up to £50,000 for railway building, but it was well aware that much of the money was going directly into share speculation. (Keen as the Bank was to promote the railways, it was less enthusiastic about a railway in its own backyard in Edinburgh. It opposed the construction of the North British Railway Company's lines through Princes Street Gardens and sold land for the purpose only when forced to do so.) The Directors became very concerned during the latter half of 1845 at the outflow from reserves and asked Andrew Neilson to provide them with a detailed report of the situation in Glasgow. His comments are worth quoting in detail.

> As desired by you we beg to report that the manufactures of this district during the whole of 1845 were generally speaking in a very sound and healthy state: the cotton spinning trade being particularly prosperous. The only exception which might perhaps be made to this observation is that of handloom manufacturers and calico printers in the export trade and in regard to them we doubt whether their foreign consignments would yield a return adequate to the increased price of the goods.
>
> The railway speculation which existed here as in every other part of the Kingdom was certainly an unfavourable feature in the transactions of the

year, but it had this effect that prices of raw productions and manufacture were generally kept low and production more moderate than it would otherwise have been. The article of iron was the only exception – in it prices vibrated greatly and much money must have been made and lost in it by speculators.

Our working population were very well employed, their wages were good and provisions cheap, their power of consumption had therefore a very favourable reflex influence upon the internal trade of the country.

As to the position of matters now, they are in several respects less favourable than they were; confidence has been so checked that the regular demand for manufactures has been much interfered with, the foreign markets are not generally in a better state, and though labourers in the formation of railways and in some other branches are well employed and at good wages, we think that the home trade generally cannot be in as favourable a position as it was twelve months ago. Add to this the rapid advance in the value of money and that at a time when railway calls and outlays otherwise arising out of the prosperous trade of last year are just beginning to operate most powerfully.

In these circumstances and with the belief that the value of money will continue high for a considerable time forward, we do not think the position of matters here so favourable as it was; at the same time we are not aware of anything in our own position involving undue risk. We have lately waived anything of this character as also transactions in which we thought the parties were too much dependent upon facilities of Banking Accommodation.

To-morrow the 3rd of March is one of the heaviest days of bill payments throughout the year and being followed by the 4th of the month (always a heavy day) we anticipate that the strength of the mercantile community will be severely tested. If the payments be well got over we think it will be a favourable feature in our prospects for some time to come.

We think the chief danger at present is with houses who are widely extended or whose paper requires to be kept uniformly up or to be turned over by extended transactions. There are few accounts in our books which seem to answer this description.

The bubble burst on 18 October 1847. Alexander Blair revealed to the Directors that to sustain the Bank's position between 1845 and 1847 it had been necessary to sell, usually at a loss, some £1,198,000 of its reserve stock, which was equal to the whole of the undivided profit. If the Bank was to continue to support lending at the same level it would be necessary to sell a further £600,000 of Government securities. The alternative was to contract credit and thereby give a further downward twist to the collapse. Glasgow was particularly badly affected and it was reckoned by one of the Directors that the crash cost £4 million, which represented 10 per cent of the banking capital of Scotland. Part of the story for industrial firms in Glasgow and Paisley was wage demands to meet rising grain prices, itself one outcome of the failure of the potato crop in Ireland and the West of

Scotland. The period of panic did not last long. The Government allowed the Bank of England to make loans freely and all the Scottish banks to exceed their authorised issue without penalty. Bank of Scotland's comparative caution in railway lending meant that the Glasgow agency suffered a loss of only £15,000 and was obliged in its central accounts to make further provision of some £12,800. Total losses of £30,000 in 1847 were very small compared with those of other banks. But events did demonstrate very clearly to Blair that the capital of the original three Scottish chartered banks would be more effective if they could combine to create a specific reserve bank for Scotland. Soundings at both the Treasury and the Bank of England produced no insurmountable obstacles to the idea, so negotiations were opened with the Royal Bank and the British Linen Company to create a single chartered bank with a combined capital of £3.5 million, a note issue of £979,483, deposits of £14 million and a network of 74 branches. The prize was a large one. The restructured Bank of Scotland would have had unrivalled leadership over the Scottish banking system; it would have yielded greater profits to the shareholders of the original three banks by restraining competition; and it would have allowed Blair's ideas about correct banking principles to be imposed upon the whole system. It would also have created one of the biggest banks in Europe and made it one of the largest players in the City of London. The project excited Government interest and in 1850 the Treasurer received a surprise visit from Sir Charles Wood, Chancellor of the Exchequer, who wished to inform himself about the Scottish banking system. In fact the idea of a combined bank faded away, probably killed in 1851 by the British Linen Company, which was 'not prepared to consider further the state of banking in Scotland till after the meeting of Parliament'.

The years between 1848 and 1854 were lean ones for business. Trade reports emphasise general caution and a lack of demand for loans. As a consequence, branch profits slumped and general policy was dictated by a need to rebuild the London reserves. Money loaned to railway companies was not withdrawn: in 1850 the Edinburgh and Glasgow Railway, for example, had its loan facility renewed for £50,000, the same amount as had been lent in 1843. In 1853 Bank of Scotland took its first steps towards 'new technology'. Head Office in Edinburgh was connected to the London agent by electric telegraph, and London Stock Exchange prices became instantly available. It was the announcement of war with Russia in 1854 which restored confidence to industry, with a huge increase in demand for the products of the Scots burghs.

—The Last Duel in Scotland,— 23 August 1826

The protagonists in the last duel fought in Scotland were the Bank of Scotland's agent in Kirkcaldy and one of the Bank's customers. David Morgan, who became the Bank's Kirkcaldy agent in 1816, was also a prominent lawyer and conducted both his own and the Bank's business from Pye's House in the Kirkwynd. In 1820 he was joined as co-agent by his son George, who was a half-pay lieutenant in the 72nd Regiment. George Morgan was an arrogant and irascible man who failed to honour customer confidentiality and publicly queried the credit-worthiness of David Langdale, a linen merchant, bleachfield owner and prominent 'Auld Lichter' in the 'lang toun'. Whether by malice or stupidity, the quarrel was allowed to grow until Morgan challenged Langdale to a duel. This was fought at Cardenbarns on 23 August 1826 and Morgan was killed. At the trial before Lord Cockburn at Perth in September, Langdale was acquitted on the grounds that he had done everything to avoid a quarrel and had therefore acted in self-defence. Among those appearing for Langdale were Archibald Bennet, the Bank Secretary, and Walter Fergus, the town's former Provost. As a result, Kirkcaldy linen manufacturers felt they were no longer well served by the Bank and transferred their business to a branch of the Union Bank of Scotland which opened under Walter Fergus in 1835. It is pleasing to record that the quarrel between the Langdales and Morgans was not long-lasting. In 1839 Alexander G. Morgan joined his uncle in the Bank agency and subsequently married David Langdale's daughter. Out of this came Langdale, Morgan & Co., jute manufacturers of Calcutta, and the beginnings of Kirkcaldy's linoleum industry.

David Langdale's duelling pistols, now in Kirkcaldy Museum

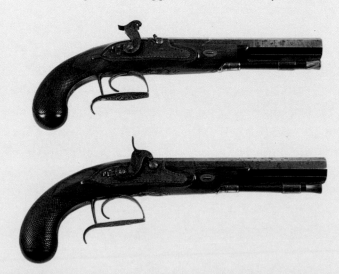

—10—

WIDER HORIZONS AND DOMESTIC PROBLEMS, 1850–95

O N 10 June 1851 the Governor – Robert, second Viscount Melville – died, breaking 75 years of continuous family service to the Bank. He was 80 years of age and had, since the events of 1832, largely withdrawn from daily and active involvement in the Bank's affairs. Lord Cockburn provided a fitting epitaph:

> After holding high offices and performing their duties well, he retired from public life about twenty years ago and has ever since resided quietly at Melville Castle. But though withdrawing from London and its great functions, he did not renounce usefulness, but entered into every Edinburgh work in which it could be employed with respectability . . . He deserved this unanimous public trust by plain manners, great industry, excellent temper, sound sense and singular fairness. There could not possibly be a better man of business.

It is a measure of the change in the management style of the Bank since 1832 that Melville's successor, Lord Dalhousie, was Governor-General of India and therefore not resident in Scotland. As President of the Board of Trade in Peel's administration he had coped well with the consequences of railway 'mania' in 1846–47. His task in India was to modernise the administration and improve communications. The grand design was to build a railway network on the subcontinent. This was to be financed by stock offering a guaranteed interest rate above British Government stock with identical security, which it was hoped would limit the opportunities for speculation. Lord Dalhousie's role was to encourage the Bank to take

James Alexander, tenth Earl and eighteenth Marquess of Dalhousie, Governor 1851-60, in the uniform of the Royal Company of Archers, by Sir John Watson Gordon (Scottish National Portrait Gallery)

investments in Indian stock and play a more active part in foreign capital investment. In one sense he was pushing at a half-open door. Bank customers in Dundee and Kirkcaldy were already becoming heavily involved in the jute trade and needed more knowledge of trading conditions to support this. Bank of Scotland's main problem was that, unlike most other Scottish banks, it had no foreign correspondents and sub-contracted all work of foreign remittance and letters of credit to Coutts or Smith, Payne and Smith in London, who found the business very profitable. In such circumstances the Bank could build up no foreign investment expertise. Alexander Blair remained sceptical about the merits of foreign correspondents in India, USA, Canada and Australia, so the matter was allowed to rest during the rest of his Treasurership.

By 1854 the Bank's now traditional views about the extension of credit and liquidity began to look seriously outmoded, and even Alexander Blair believed that a more adventurous investment and lending policy was justified. The reasons for a change of direction were presented in 1855 in a report to the Directors, who were most impressed by the fact that a bank with a capital base similar to that of Bank of Scotland (unnamed, but probably the Union Bank of Scotland) could create profits of £130,000, some £40,000 more than the Bank's profits for 1854. This difference was the direct result of using £1 million of deposits to discount commercial bills in Glasgow. The Board also noted that the Bank was at a disadvantage in attracting Glasgow business because it had no resident support among merchants and manufacturers, and they seriously considered setting up a Glasgow board of directors. The final decision was that there should eventually be three new branches in Glasgow, with new loans being negotiated either by the Glasgow manager or by the agent of the new branch at Laurieston, the only one which was actually opened in 1855. These were to report to Edinburgh and be inspected in the traditional way. This expansion required £500,000 in extra deposits and permitted additional loans of £850,000 while still allowing £3,505,000 for the Glasgow bill trade. Business expanded rapidly among West of Scotland manufacturers and traders and this was also extended to England. All the Scottish banks, with the exception of the British Linen Company, pursued a similar course of action.

The backcloth against which this happened was a very rapid growth in the British economy and in overseas trade. Between 1845 and 1855 British manufactured exports rose by some 62 per cent. Both self-confidence and pride in achievement were boosted by the success of the Great Exhibition at London's Crystal Palace in 1851; and the feeling of general prosperity

Dundee, weaving at Mid-Wynd Jute Works, 1850 (Dundee Museum and Art Gallery)

was enhanced by the discovery of gold in California in 1849. Although Alexander Blair was uncertain about the effect of an increased gold supply on commodity prices in Britain, it was a matter for regular review rather than serious worry.

In the first four months of 1857 the general economic position began to deteriorate and the Bank began to draw back on its lending for fear of becoming over-extended. The twenty-five years of Blair's stewardship had shifted the balance of the Bank's business very significantly. In 1832 deposits in the Bank had been £3,188,000, advances in Scotland £1,970,000 and reserves in London £2,035,000. In 1857 deposits were £5,327,000 and advances £4,390,000, while London reserves stood at £2,140,536. After certain allowances were made, this gave the Bank a convertible reserve of £1,530,536. If Blair's own principles about reserves had been followed, the convertible reserve in 1857 should have stood at £1,800,000. The ratio of reserves to liabilities had been set at 1:3 at a Board meeting of 30 November 1840, and so there was a shortfall of some £269,464. In other words, the structure of the Bank's business was increasingly similar to that of its competitors, from which followed the obvious corollary that it was no longer in a position to act as a quasi-reserve bank for the whole Scottish system. That opportunity had been lost with the rejection of Blair's amalgamation plans in the 1840s. In view of what was to follow, it was ironic that the public perception of Bank of Scotland's

Photograph of Head Office, the Mound, c.1850, from Waverley Station

proper role remained that of an earlier generation.

The crisis gathered momentum during the summer of 1857. News of the mutiny of a number of regiments in the East India Company in northern India and the subsequent massacres of British subjects reached London in July, and a number of small American banks began to close. By mid-October the trickle had become a flood: all but one of the 63 New York houses closed; and trade to the USA was severely curtailed. Prices of manufactured goods awaiting shipment from Britain began to fall and the Bank of England added to the problem by raising its discount rate from 5.5 to 8 per cent within a period of ten days in October. There were even more bank failures in the USA: some 1,415 banks were shut during October, with total liabilities of $299,810,000. By early November many industrial companies and merchant houses, particularly in Liverpool and Glasgow, suspended payments and laid off workers. Crucially, the Dennistoun business, with interests in Glasgow, Liverpool, London, New York and New Orleans, stopped payments. There was a crisis of confidence in Glasgow, leading to runs on the Western Bank, the City of Glasgow Bank and the Union Bank of Scotland; but all Scottish banks were affected, apart from the British Linen Company and the Dundee Banking Company. On 9 November the Western Bank and the City of Glasgow Bank closed their doors.

The Western Bank had, since its founding in 1832, been consistently

Panoramic view of Edinburgh, 1868

opposed to the sound banking principles advocated by Blair and had considered that £20,000 to £25,000 in London reserves was more than sufficient for the conduct of its business. There had been problems in 1834 and 1847 and from these the Western carried an overhang of bad and doubtful debt for which no provision had been made. In 1854 this was estimated to be £420,000, equal to four years' annual dividend. This was not publicly known. By July 1857, after writing off £125,000 of bad debts, £327,000 of debts remained as 'hopeless'. If US debts and their impact on the Glasgow scene were taken into consideration, the total problem was believed to amount to £1,603,726. During October the Bank and the Royal, together with the Union, Commercial and National banks, put up £600,000 as an initial safety net, but on the 19th news of this was leaked to *The Times*, and customers' deposits were withdrawn from the Western. The Bank of England refused to intervene and would not suspend the Bank Charter Act to permit Bank of England notes to circulate in Scotland. On 10 and 11 November £1 million of gold was moved north and the military placed on full alert. Bank of Scotland has consistently received a bad press for its actions during this crisis. In fact, the books reveal that its support for the Western Bank cost £413,500 which, when added to support for other banks in difficulty, amounted to a total support operation costing £874,000 by the first week of December 1857.

Predictably, the Bank's own customers had problems and they had first call on its resources. It has been calculated that by the end of 1857 Bank of Scotland had moved a total of £2,173,000 from its reserves to increase liquidity. Had not new deposits of £500,000 been forthcoming during November and December 1857, total Bank reserves would have shrunk to £300,000 at the start of 1858, a dangerously inadequate base for sound banking. Support from the Edinburgh banks was sufficient to allow the City of Glasgow Bank to reopen on 14 December, while both the Union Bank and the Edinburgh and Glasgow Bank were helped to weather the storm. So far as the Western Bank was concerned, the funds of depositors were guaranteed, and by January 1858 all business accounts and loans had been honoured. Even so, the shareholders forfeited the whole of their capital and Glaswegians felt that Bank of Scotland could have done more.

The entire episode revealed brutally to the Scottish banks that they were now regarded as bit players on the financial scene, particularly since it demonstrated to English commentators the value of the 1844 Act. Scots ideas about banking were unreliable and their behaviour un-British. *The Times* spoke for most articulate judges south of the Border on the Western Bank: 'An attack upon our currency system from representatives of a concern which with eight millions of British capital entrusted to its care has brought itself to bankruptcy by fostering a set of fraudulent traders to the damage of legitimate merchants . . .' Public opinion in Glasgow preferred to believe that the whole episode was yet another example of Edinburgh mean-spiritedness, determined to do down the entrepreneurial skills of the city. Bank of Scotland's accounts reveal that the Western Bank's collapse came closer to pulling down the entire banking structure in

Left: *Silver arm-plate worn by the Bank messenger, 1840-60*
Right: *Photograph of Alexander Blair, Treasurer 1832-59*

132 Scotland than could be publicly admitted.

The events of 1857 took a heavy toll on Alexander Blair, although their immediate effects were by no means as bad as he had feared. He was in declining health for most of 1858. After preparing the Bank's submission for the Parliamentary Inquiry into the Western Bank he had to be content to sit on the sidelines while the Deputy Governor, Sir George Clerk of Penicuik, made the presentation. No new initiatives resulted from the Inquiry and in the eyes of the Board of Trade, presided over by W.E. Gladstone, the Scots system was discredited. It was a severe blow to Bank of Scotland's morale. The Bank had to rebuild its reserves and public trust in the banking system; yet at the same time Blair knew perfectly well that there was no legislation or group sanction in place which could prevent any other bank from operating in precisely the same way as the Western.

Alexander Blair died in office in February 1859 and was succeeded as Treasurer by John Mackenzie, who had previously been manager of the Scottish Widows Fund. Blair's efforts brought the Bank through the crisis in good shape, and recovery was rapid. By 1860 Bank of Scotland possessed some 43 branches, of which only five had been taken over from the Western Bank, and deposits rose rapidly. The Earl of Dalhousie's interests in India bore fruit in 1859, when the Bank tendered for £150,000 worth of British India debentures. It was during this operation that John Mackenzie began to look hard at the commission taken and at non-interest-bearing cash deposits carried by the Bank's London corresponding banks, Coutts and Smith Payne's. He reckoned that in total this cost the Bank £5,256 a year. One particular area for concern was that all Scottish banks were finding it increasingly difficult either to lend money or to obtain first-class secure bills in London.

Although Britain was not directly involved in any major wars during the 1860s, the export business was affected by a number of changes in Europe. The Franco-Austrian War of 1859–60 began the process which was to lead to Italian unification. The German empire, dominated by Prussian interests, was created in a series of wars with Denmark and Austria and finally in 1870 with France. It was, however, the American Civil War, with its consequent restriction of raw cotton exports from the Southern States, which hastened the decline of the cotton industry in the West of Scotland. Its eventual replacements – modern steelmaking and shipbuilding – were in their infancy. Bank profits fell from £150,000 in 1861 to £115,000 in 1862 and 1863. By 1865 they were down to £80,000.

It became clear to the Directors that if lending opportunities in the West of Scotland were to become more restricted, new outlets for

Above: *One of Peddie and Kinnear's alternative treatments for the north elevation of Head Office, the Mound, 1859-61*

Right and below: *David Bryce's plan and south elevation for Head Office, the Mound, 1864-70*

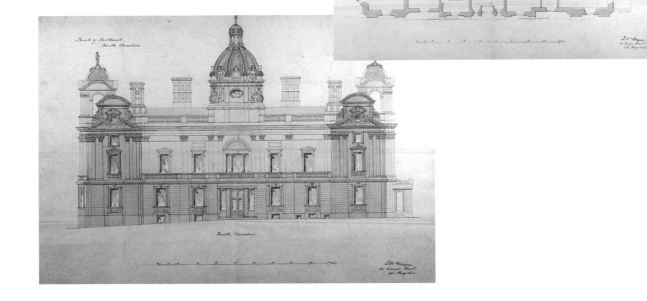

134   investment were required. This was a direction in which the Treasurer, John Mackenzie, felt his inexperience, and the pressures of the situation aggravated his ill-health. He wisely decided to step down in 1863 on health grounds, although he was to live until 1901 and serve as a director of the Union Bank of Scotland from 1887. His successor was David Davidson, who after apprenticeship in Scotland had become manager of the Bank of Montreal, a 'Scots' bank very familiar with the activities of Scots in Canada's West and North West Territories. His experience of land settlement and investment in new territories was invaluable to the Bank, and his period of office to 1879 signalled an advance of the Bank's efforts on every front.

The most obvious change was that work began almost immediately on extending the Bank's Head Office on the Mound in Edinburgh. This was a project which had been under consideration for over fifteen years. In 1850, in response both to criticism from Edinburgh residents that the Bank presented its ugly back to the New Town and to the need for additional accommodation, the Bank had commissioned drawings from the architect Thomas Hamilton. His proposal was to extend the Bank sideways to the east and west with a pair of pavilions linked to the earlier building and to place the main entrance of the Bank on the north side facing the New Town. Architecturally the main problem was that Hamilton stuck to a 'Georgian' appearance, and although he could get the building to look balanced from either the north *or* the south side, his design did not allow both to appear in proportion. In fact the project was abandoned after preliminary discussions and was never costed. In 1859–61 the Edinburgh architects Peddie & Kinnear prepared a portfolio of alternative treatments of the exterior, based on a near-identical ground plan. These varied from Greek temple, through French château to Victorian Gothic railway station. It is probable that the Directors and Treasurer took fright, but in 1864 the architect David Bryce was commissioned and his designs were carried out between 1864 and 1870. His solution was neat and very satisfying. In effect he encased the original building in a new shell and added two new wings, which emphasised the vertical lines of the Old Town building but broke up the sheer mass with horizontal elements of decoration. Internally, a two-storey entrance and banking hall were created with offices and two domestic flats. The original dome was extended upwards and topped by a statue of Fame, balanced by two smaller, lower cupolas, also with statues.

For the whole period of the remodelling, the Head Office staff worked on in the middle of a building site. When the building account was closed in 1875 some £43,500 had been spent on the alterations, but at the Annual

General Meeting of 1870 Davidson had told the Proprietors that Head Office on the Mound would not stand in the Bank's books at more than £30,000. The way in which this was done is an interesting example of the attitudes to property values in the Victorian age compared with the present day. In a Board minute of 28 December 1858 it was agreed that a general property account would be created in which rents received for the Bank's let property would be set against expenditure, with only the balance being carried to the general accounts. The other decision was to take a sum of money out of the net profit each year before the declaration of the Proprietors' dividend, to 'the reduction of the heritable property in the occupation of the Bank'. Between 1861 and 1891 this amounted to £5,000 a year and tended to be set against the costs of new or refurbished buildings. In other words, property values were depreciated each year. Up to 1880 the Bank Head Office on the Mound had cost £96,229 to build. By 1910 it had no value as an asset in the Bank's accounts.

This was not the only building work carried out. In 1860 the Bank had 43 branches, but by 1880 this had risen to 106. Of this additional number only 15 were taken over from other banks. Even with a policy of writing down costs, the value of property recorded on the Bank's annual balance sheet rose from around £83,000 in 1860 to £249,021 in 1880, a three-fold increase in just twenty years. As a proportion of the Bank's total assets it rose by 50 per cent, a clear indication of the speed of expansion under

Central Bank of Scotland £1 note
'pull' from a steel-engraved plate

Left: *David Davidson, Treasurer 1862-79*
Right: *James Wenley, Treasurer 1879-98, taken about 1881*

Above: *Bank of Scotland notes of the 1860s and 1870s*
Foot: *Experimental £100 note of 1880 (never issued)*

David Davidson. In addition to changes at Head Office other major building works were carried out at Beauly, Falkirk, Aberdeen, New Cumnock, Oban and St Andrews, while in Glasgow a new principal office was built between 1865 and 1869 at 1 St Vincent Place at a cost of £48,654.

The expansion of the Scottish banks into England began when the National Bank opened an office in London. The problem remained the Bank of England's charter; and during 1865 Bank of Scotland, the British Linen Company, the Clydesdale and the Union Bank of Scotland prepared a scheme for a jointly owned bank, the London and Scottish Banking Association, with a capital of £3 million and limited liability. The intention was to channel all Scots investment business through the new bank. The project collapsed in 1866, and Bank of Scotland decided to establish its own London office. Premises were leased at 11 Old Broad Street at an annual rental of £3,430 and opened for business on 16 April 1867. To the surprise of the Bank's Directors, the London branch had taken over £400,000 of deposits by 1869, and a move to new rented premises at 43 Lothbury in 1870 provided much-needed business space. By 1871 London deposits had reached £900,000 and the potential for lending to London Scots was very large. The net profit of the London branch had reached £3,500 after only three years of business.

The success of the London office both justified and confirmed David Davidson's instincts about the disabilities that Scots banks faced in London if they operated through agents. First, with the growth in the social importance of the London 'Season', aristocratic customers preferred to deal with a London-based bank, even if the bulk of their income was derived from Scottish estates or businesses. Good business was being lost. Secondly, the Scottish banks were only getting access to London bills and lending after others had taken first pick. Thirdly, they were paying handsomely for the privilege of being second-best in London. Finally, it was clear that there was a strong latent demand among London Scots for Scottish banking facilities.

In 1868 the Bank took over seven of the branches of the Central Bank of Scotland, a Perth-based concern founded in 1834. At various times of crisis during the 1840s and '50s it had been assisted by Bank of Scotland and by 1868 owed a total of £52,000. The solution was to buy the bank outright by offering Central Bank shareholders Bank of Scotland stock held either in reserves or in the pension fund. A minority of the shareholders were reluctant to sell, so the Central Bank had a nominal independence for a further 12 years, when those surviving were bought out by a payment of £2 3s. per share. It was a good purchase, with large

138 deposits, and gave Bank of Scotland a secure footing among the farmers and landowners of Perthshire.

In 1873 it began to seem probable that the Bank's expansion would be restricted by its authorised capital, which had been set at £1.5 million in 1804, although up to 1872 only £1 million had been called up. The new Act of 1873 authorised a capital of £4.5 million, which appeared to meet needs as far ahead as anyone could see. In fact, only £250,000 was called up from the Proprietors in 1876 and the Bank's paid-up capital remained at £1.25 million until 1907. Unlike the Union Bank and the Clydesdale, Bank of Scotland was able to support its continued expansion from within its reserves without making calls on its Proprietors.

In 1875 Scottish banking faced a serious challenge to its intention to expand into the English market. The Chancellor, Sir Stafford Northcote, was determined to remove existing Scots banks from England, and a Parliamentary Committee of Inquiry was set up. There were several threads to his thinking. Firstly, the Scottish banks tended to work together, and with their large capital funds they provided increasingly strong competition in London. Secondly, there had been a steady stream of complaints that the 1845 Act had given the Scots banks an unfair advantage. Thirdly, from 1874 the industrial boom of the previous decade was over and all banks and bill brokers were looking for good, secure investments. The desire of Scottish banks (and English joint-stock banks) to move into the profitable 'acceptance' business challenged the role of city brokers and bankers, who presented this expansion as a direct challenge to the authority of the Bank of England. It is notable that among the chief advocates of restricting the Scottish banks was the South Essex MP, Thomas Charles Baring, in a happy coincidence of private interest and public duty. George Joachim Goschen, MP for the City of London, emphasised the point that Scots banks moving to London could keep their bank-note issue in Scotland, but that English banks moving to Scotland could not issue Bank of England notes 'because people will not take them'. In fact, for once, the Scots banks underestimated the eagerness of London interests to expel them. The Scots case was not presented with sufficient robustness and clarity. One of the features which most strongly told against them was that they appeared to be operating in concert, as a cartel, consolation to a swathe of investors, mostly in Glasgow, who were made bankrupt. James Wenley was the Bank of Scotland's main representative in the subsequent clear-up. As in 1857, the prime consideration was the banking system as a whole. Deposits and loans were honoured, and the bulk of the branch system, with its existing staff, was taken over by the Royal Bank. Bank of Scotland acquired just eight branches. One additional complication was that many of the City of Glasgow Bank's agents had also been shareholders and a number were personally bankrupt. In one or two cases Bank of Scotland could help. The manager of the Edinburgh branch in Hanover Street was appointed Cashier of Bank of Scotland, which gave him a flat in the Bank House on the Mound, and his salary was publicly designated as 'allowances'. The collapse of the City of Glasgow Bank scarred a generation of Scots bankers and was the worst crisis to hit the Scots business community in the second half of the nineteenth century. One long-term consequence of these events was that over the next ten years there was a raft of legislation limiting the personal liability of shareholders and dealing with company structure and bookkeeping. In banking the 1882 Cheque Act and the Bankers Book Evidence Act 1881 are still extant in 1995 and dictate record-keeping practices. Independent auditing of company accounts, registration of companies, and publication of annual results in a standard form were required by the 1879 Companies Act. It is interesting to note that the names of the Bank's auditors appear in the Annual Report for the first time in 1879. That year's Annual Report is also unusual in that it contains two pages of remarks on the crisis by the Governor. The Annual Report reverted the following year to a simpler format which was basically unchanged until 1946, when a profit and loss account was added for the first time.

When David Davidson retired in May 1879 in ill-health, one major effect of the worries of the previous year, the clear choice of Bank of Scotland's Directors as his successor was James Wenley. Many of Davidson's initiatives in colonial business were steadily bearing fruit. Important companies became customers, and a series of corresponding agents was established in Canada, Australia, New Zealand and South Africa. Increased knowledge of conditions made it possible for the Bank to widen the scope of its investment book, and in 1878 US government bonds and New South Wales government debentures were bought for the first time.

James Wenley's 19 years as Treasurer were very mixed ones for the Bank. On the one hand it regained its position as Scotland's first bank, a matter which owed much to David Davidson's groundwork. On the other hand the general economy of Scotland remained in depression during

142   much of the 1880s and the collaboration which had been a normal feature of Scottish banking became a rigid system in which banks did not poach customers from each other, matched interest rates and were in general very cautious. The changes in the Bank's business were the subject of a detailed report prepared by James Gourlay, the Bank's Glasgow manager, for James Wenley in 1894. His summary was as follows:

> The above will show that the conditions under which business is conducted in Glasgow are much more difficult now than they were twenty years ago, and that the profits of banks show a downward tendency . . .

In fact he was describing what had emerged during the 1860s and 1870s as a distinctive geographical pattern in the Bank's business. The spread of branches into new middle-class suburbs and country towns, 123 by 1895, meant that in Scotland most were taking in deposits almost twice as great as the sums of money lent. The significance of the Glasgow and Laurieston branches was that they were the prime channels through which the Bank's lending business was conducted. After 1889 the surplus on this process had to be placed in bills and securities through the London office. The difficulties of finding profitable opportunities for lending is a constant theme of the 1880s and 1890s. In 1883 the Bank contemplated, in defiance of the 'agreement' of 1875, opening a second London branch in the West End. It was hoped that this would become a channel for lending, but in fact the idea was dropped when it became clear that it too would become a channel for deposit-taking rather than lending. The question must be asked whether the Bank was over-cautious in its lending policies. The whole underlying theme of Gourlay's report is a defence of the role of the Glasgow office, which over the 15 years since 1879 had resulted in some £102,000 being written off the Bank's lending book. The view from the Mound suggested that a cavalier policy was in place rather than the reverse. Some detailed figures illustrate the crucial points better than many words.

		1869	1894	Increase
A	**Deposits** (Bank)	8,400,000	14,700,000	6,650,000
	Deposits (Glasgow Chief Office)	650,000	2,000,000	1,350,000
	Deposits (Glasgow and Glasgow Branches)	1,000,000	2,750,000	1,750,000

Some Bank of Scotland Agents in the 1880s and 1890s

144 B **Loans at Glasgow Chief Office**

	On Bills	On Cash Credits	On Overdrafts	Loans on Stock	
1869	1,250,000	350,000	150,000	-	1,750,000
1894	1,450,000	500,000	1,300,000	500,000	3,750,000
				Increase	2,000,000

It can be seen that in 1869 Glasgow Chief Office's deposits covered only 30 per cent of loans, but by 1894, if the other Glasgow branches are taken into consideration, they covered 73 per cent of lending. Most significant of all was the change from lending on a bill with a fixed time limit to lending on overdraft, in theory instantly recoverable but in practice a running account whose limits were adjusted according to the business concerned. The implication is clear and fits with the deposit evidence. During the 1880s and '90s most of the Bank's large business customers in the West generated their capital requirements from internal profits and looked to the Bank to cover cash flow variations. Gourlay also stated that the cash credit had simply become unfashionable among customers and there were fewer bills because people preferred to pay cash and take an extra discount on their purchases. There is very little doubt that most of the Bank's new connections in the period came from Glasgow and were widely spread across the whole range of business in the West of Scotland. Of its rivals only the National Bank came close, while of the two Glasgow-based banks the Union Bank of Scotland slipped in rank order and the Clydesdale maintained its 1869 position. The outcome of the Board discussions which followed Gourlay's report was to keep the policies in place but to be on the look-out for new businesses and industries which might offer increased lending opportunities.

Between 1891 and 1893 the focus of the Bank's concerns shifted to London. The business of the London branch was very distinctive. Such advances as were made were to corporations, public bodies, other bankers, bill brokers and stockbrokers. Private customers were Scottish firms which preferred to pass their bills via London. In other words, it was a specialised business which did not rely on private customers.

In 1891 the lease on the Bank's premises in Lothbury expired and it was made clear that the landlord required possession of the property. Several sites were reported on and the Bank's architect, G.W.T. Gwyther, suggested that offices at 'Bishopsgate within' be bought for £120,000. The earlier buildings on the site had included Crosby Hall, occupied for a number of years by Sir Thomas More, Henry VIII's Chancellor. In one of those curious circles in the Bank's story this had been the meeting place in

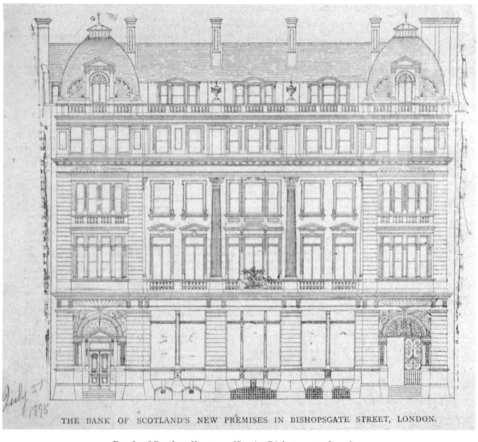

THE BANK OF SCOTLAND'S NEW PREMISES IN BISHOPSGATE STREET, LONDON.

Bank of Scotland's new office in Bishopsgate, London,
as illustrated in a newspaper report

the eighteenth century of the East India Company. In 1894 the building was demolished and a new office erected, now known as 30 Bishopsgate, which opened its doors on 25 April 1896. The London manager tended not to follow the traditional banking career of most Scottish bankers because the skills were specialised and the business unusual. From 1873 to 1899 the London manager was Robert Davidson, who had been trained in the Bank of England and who was able to build up good relations within the City and to handle the investment business.

The relationships between the Bank, the Bank of England and the City were severely tested during the Baring crisis of 1891. News was received that the City house of Baring Brothers & Company was unable to meet its liabilities, amounting to £21 million. The Scottish reaction was to treat the crisis as an English matter which the City should be left to sort out in precisely the same way that the Scots had had to sort out the City of Glasgow débâcle in 1878. Robert Davidson made it clear to the Board in Edinburgh that much more was at stake. A great swathe of investment in

146   South America was at risk, as were the City of London's credibility and the Government's own international standing. A parochial attitude would not be tolerated by the Bank of England. By the time Barings was reconstituted in 1894, each of the Scottish banks had guaranteed £300,000, while the Government provided £2 million and the Bank of England £1 million. Three London joint-stock banks provided £750,000 each, and two others £500,000. It is a measure of the changes in English banking since the 1860s that the available resources of Bank of Scotland, biggest in its own kailyard, were overtaken by no fewer than five London-based banks.

The years from 1891 to 1894 continued the depression in the coal, iron, jute and sugar industries. The Bank made two large loans to cane sugar producers in Trinidad, and from time to time an official was sent out to report on progress, a pleasant change from the normal routine of branch banking.

It looked as though trade, on the domestic front at least, would begin to improve during 1894, and the Treasurer hoped to signal better times at the Bank's bicentenary by increasing the dividend to shareholders and providing a bonus for all staff. Towards the end of the year there was a further downturn in trade, however, with a number of major customer losses being written off. In the words of Charles Malcolm, 'The 200th anniversary had thus to pass unhonoured and unsung in a year that was worse than any for a decade.'

—11—

THE UNION BANK OF SCOTLAND, 1843–1914

O F all the banks which were to become part of Bank of Scotland's twentieth-century inheritance, the Union Bank of Scotland was the most unusual in the manner of its formation. It represented the amalgamation or absorption of no fewer than 12 separate banks in different parts of Scotland, each with a distinctive history and place in its respective community. The core around which the bank developed was the Glasgow Union Banking Company, Glasgow's first joint-stock as distinct from partnership bank, which opened for business in 1830. The prime mover was the merchant Robert Stewart who, with a number of like-minded Glasgow businessmen, proposed a joint-stock bank with a nominal capital of £2 million, divided into 8,000 shares of £250 each. Their motives are made crystal clear in the first paragraph of the prospectus, which was issued on 1 January 1830:

> Seventy years have elapsed since a Native Bank was first established in this City, and during the long interval between 1760 and 1829, the population of Glasgow has increased from 25,000 to 200,000 souls; while its Manufactures, Shipping, and General Trade have increased in a much higher ratio. Accordingly, the three local Banking Establishments of this City (which have in all not more than thirty Partners) have proved so inadequate to answer the demand for Bank accommodation, that, no fewer than nine Branches of Banks, not indigenous to Glasgow, have been introduced to supply the deficiency, and are now in such active operation, as to engross a very large proportion of her Banking business. Thus have *others* been allowed to reap those profits, which, had her own citizens been more active, and more alive to their own interests, would have been realised by themselves.

Panorama of Glasgow Trongate in 1839 (Glasgow City Libraries)

Not only, however, are the citizens of Glasgow excluded from participating in the *Bank's Profits* created by their own trade, and in a great measure at the mercy of strangers for their bank accommodation, but they have, besides, been for some time back, subjected to great inconvenience, and very many of them to great loss, by the removal of almost all the Branch Banks, from the Eastern and Centre to the Western portion of the City. The waste of time thus occasioned to Merchants in the Middle and Eastern Districts, by being compelled to proceed to Virginia Street, Queen Street, or the New Exchange, to transact their Bank business, is a very serious evil, and one universally felt.

Despite the rigours of New Year, the issue was oversubscribed, so that the bank was able to pick and choose its shareholders. By 21 January, with 4,221 shares subscribed, including 1,000 which had been allocated for distribution in Edinburgh, the list was closed and the Interim Committee of Management was able to confirm that the bank would commence trading as soon as possible. A series of meetings at the beginning of February in the Tontine Building at Glasgow Cross settled the details of staffing, bank-note production and premises, and the first formal directors' meeting took place on 16 February. The first appointment was James A. Anderson as general manager. This caused some misgivings because he was a merchant, not a trained banker, but it was balanced by the appointment of William Mitchell as his deputy and cashier who *was*. The bank opened for business in premises in Post Office Court, 14 Trongate, Glasgow, in October 1830. That

Office of the Glasgow and Union Bank, 114 Trongate, Glasgow

One of a set of late eighteenth-century boardroom chairs, used by the Thistle Bank and then by the Union Bank of Scotland

same month the management was completed by the appointment of John Smith of the Aberdeen and County Bank as secretary. Perhaps the two most important decisions taken by the directors were, first, to establish a branch in Edinburgh and, second, to institute an Edinburgh committee of shareholders to supervise operations. Another innovation was a standardised five-tier system of designating customers from 'very bad', through 'bad', 'very fair', 'very good' to the supreme accolade, 'undoubted'. In their first report the directors were able to report that with a number of minor exceptions the bank had been favourably received in both Glasgow and Edinburgh. During the 1830s and unlike its younger competitors, the Western Bank and the City of Glasgow Bank, it concentrated on steady growth: by 1836 14 branches had been established compared with the 30 or so set up by the Western Bank between 1832 and 1838. The published results suggest the careful addition of new business, and lending was cautious. It was rare for a credit of more than £1,000 to be

Union Bank of Scotland Main Office, 1841-43, fronting Virginia Street,
by David Hamilton

sanctioned. It was 1838 before the bank had sufficient confidence to lend £28,000 to a railway company. The first lending on overdraft to John Leadbetter, one of the bank directors, was not agreed until 1841. As with the business, so with the return to shareholders. The dividend was increased from £7.50 to £12.50 per share over the same period. The original prospectus had stated that the bank would remain in the Trongate area of Glasgow. It was therefore with great heart-searching that in 1833 the Union Bank followed the westward march of Glasgow's business district to new premises at the head of Virginia Street.

In 1836 the Union Bank began what was over the next twenty years to become a habit of absorption and amalgamation. During the course of three weeks in June, with three meetings and two exchanges of letters, the assets and liabilities of the Glasgow-based Thistle Bank were taken over at valuation. During 1838 two additions were made: the Paisley Union Bank and Sir William Forbes and Company, Edinburgh's last surviving private banker. In the former case the partners were eager to retire and the terms agreed revolved around the size of annuities and the issue of Union Bank stock. There were only three partners, and the settlement gave each an annuity of £2,500 for ten years and 50 Union Bank shares.

In many ways the most significant takeover was that of Sir William Forbes and Company. The great days of private bankers were past, and the firm had been steadily losing its traditional business to either the National Bank of Scotland or the three chartered banks. The basis of negotiation was the net profit of £16,000 made during 1836. A close examination of the books

indicated that this was an above-average year for profits, and the figure was 151
reduced to £10,666, which was accepted by the Edinburgh partners, provided
that it was guaranteed. The remaining un-issued Union Bank stock was given
to them, and the remaining sum was made up with annuities. The partners
undertook to continue the management of the Edinburgh business for six
years (when their own co-partnery agreement would expire), and Charles
Forbes, grandson of Sir William Forbes of Pitsligo (see Chapter 6), undertook
to live in Glasgow to work towards the full integration of the two banks.

At no point were Union Bank shareholders permitted to know the exact
terms of the agreement and they were barely content with the assurance that
discussion would be 'highly inexpedient and objectionable'. When during
1843 it became clear that both the Glasgow and Ship Bank and Hunters and
Company of Ayr were to be amalgamated with the bank, it was decided that
a new company structure was required. The actual document forming the
Union Bank of Scotland in 1843 is one of the most extraordinary in all
Scottish banking. It is in the form of a roll
nearly 15 metres long, one-third of which
contains the articles of agreement and the
remainder the signature of every single
shareholder. Being no longer 'a local bank in
the City of Glasgow', the Union Bank

Banking Company in Aberdeen bank-note
after amalgamation with the Union Bank
Below: *Castle Street, Aberdeen, in the 1820s.*
The Bank is on the right of the picture

established two head offices, one in Glasgow and one in Edinburgh, with six directors resident in each city, a system of regional organisation which, suitably modified, persists into the 1990s and is one of Bank of Scotland's legacies from the Union Bank. The paid-up capital of the older Glasgow and Union Bank stood at £500,000, although the nominal capital stood at £2.5 million. Since the paid-up capital of the Glasgow and Ship Bank also stood at £500,000, a decision was taken to keep the paid-up capital of the Union Bank of Scotland at £1 million divided into £50 shares, while the nominal capital was set at £2 million.

The combined effect of these amalgamations is best illustrated in a table prepared by the Japanese scholar Norio Tamaki, which is reproduced in simplified form on page 158.

Seven years of amalgamations resulted in the creation of a formidable bank with a national spread of branches, a large fund of goodwill and a wide range of business. The full absorption of Sir William Forbes & Co. into the Union Bank did not take place until 1846, when the original Edinburgh partners retired. The new Edinburgh manager, Samuel Hay, appointed at a salary of £800 a year, was quickly accepted as an honoured and trusted member of the Edinburgh financial community. The Edinburgh office became the base for control of circulation and coin.

Between 1844 and 1857 two further takeovers gave the Union Bank its final shape; and there were two attempted takeovers, of the Dundee Bank in 1849 and of the Caledonian Bank in 1851 and 1856, both of which failed.

The Aberdeen Banking Company, which agreed to be taken over in 1849, was in very poor shape. It had a large overhang of bad and doubtful debts, the largest of which was the Banner Mill, alone estimated at £35,340. This bank had had a chequered career over the previous twenty years which had reduced its capital to £7,047, divided into 34,235 shares. It has to be said that the Union Bank mounted a rescue operation. Shareholders were offered £2 per Aberdeen Banking Company share in Union Bank stock priced at £80 a share. That is to say, 40 Aberdeen Banking Company shares were exchanged for one Union Bank share. An attempt in 1849 to bid for the Perth Banking Company was rejected. But by 1857 the Perth partners had changed their minds and come to the conclusion that increased competition for business forced them to look for a marriage with a larger bank. The paid-up shares of £100,050 were valued at £2 each and were once again offered in exchange for Union Bank stock. With a number of minor financial adjustments the terms were accepted, and on 27 February 1858 the Perth Bank name disappeared from the office in St John Street, Perth and from 11 other branches in Perthshire.

During the 1840s and '50s the Union Bank of Scotland, despite policies that were very much in the spirit of Glasgow enterprise, never attracted the criticism of its peers. Between 1844 and 1858 the bank's total liabilities grew by *140 per cent*. Two arms of business distinguished it from the Edinburgh banks. First, it moved into 'acceptances' (bills of exchange) in the late 1840s and became heavily involved in the American and Australian trade of J.A. Dennistoun and Company, whose trade account stood at £400,000 in October 1853. Word of mouth ensured that the international business connections of Dennistoun's also provided new business, and it has been calculated that this was one of the main engines of the Union Bank's expansion in the period. Loans were made to the Tennants of St Rollox Chemical Works in Glasgow, and to the Monkland Iron and Steel Co.; and in 1855 a credit of £20,000 was granted for the first time to J. & G. Thomson, Shipbuilders, a firm which under various names was to feature regularly in the Union Bank's lending book down to 1955. The second area was railway finance, where loans were made almost entirely on the security of railway stock or debentures. These loans were usually for six months, but could be for up to two to three years.

The early years of the 1850s saw the Union Bank open an account with the Bank of England, develop a portfolio of railway stock and commit itself to foreign trade financing. Accounts were opened with Dennistoun contacts in New York, Paris and India. A significant proportion of the bank's 'formal' portfolio was invested in its own stock, and indeed the directors were encouraged to buy up stock whenever the price showed any signs of decline. In parallel with this development, branch formation accelerated

Glasgow in the 1860s

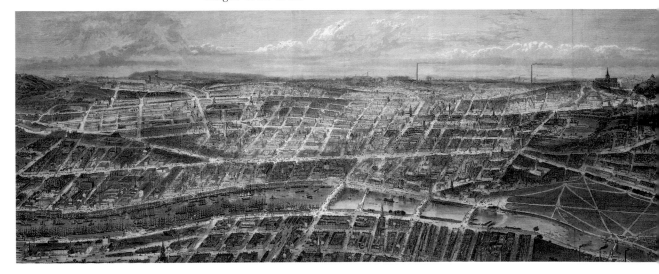

154 and by 1858 the network contained 99 branches: this was part of the policy of James Robertson, who succeeded James Anderson as manager in 1852, and it meant that the Union Bank topped the league table.

In 1857 the crisis which led to the closure of the Western Bank also severely affected the Union Bank. The failure of Carr, Josling & Co. of London had a severe knock-on effect and the firm of Dennistoun & Co. collapsed and had to stop business. Dennistoun's had a widespread international business, particularly in America, and had over-extended its trading. Alexander Dennistoun was a director of the bank and, as indicated earlier, the firm was almost certainly its largest customer. There was a run on the Union Bank during 10 and 11 November, but the Bank of England and the Edinburgh banks were able to provide help. Despite this, the price of Union Bank stock plummeted as the public perceived just how completely the Union was thirled to Dennistoun's. In the event, and with a little help from its friends, the Union Bank survived, but the experience provoked an examination of its policies and a change of direction.

In the eyes of the Edinburgh directors, James Robertson had been largely to blame for the near disaster of 1857. A young accountant called Charles Gairdner, who had been assistant liquidator of the Western Bank and a founding member of the Institute of Accountants and Actuaries in Glasgow in 1855, was asked in 1861 to carry out an investigation and to report on the Union Bank's structure and balance sheet. This revealed a range of problems and in 1862 Gairdner was appointed joint general manager, becoming sole manager in 1865 when James Robertson retired. He joined the bank board in 1865 and remained until his retiral in 1895. Quite apart from the performance of his duties as general manager, he was one of the foremost writers on banking theory in nineteenth-century Scotland and therefore had an influence on banking far beyond the confines of Glasgow.

Charles Gairdner's period at the Union Bank saw the implementation of cautious lending policies and much tighter management of the bank. The most significant change of all was the outcome of a review of investments which resulted in a much higher percentage of assets being carried as Consols and other Government securities. The consequence of all this was that between 1866 and 1879 the Union Bank fell continuously in ranking among the Scottish banks in terms of total liabilities, deposits and advances; even its branch network was overtaken by others. The policy of caution in these years was reinforced by two major failures which impacted on the bank's assets. The failure of the bank Overend, Gurney and Co. in 1866 led to an eventual loss of £26,000; although worrying, this was not serious. The fraudulent collapse in 1875 of

Charles Gairdner, General Manager of the Union Bank 1865-95
Staff of the Law Department, Union Bank, c.1900

Alexander Collie and Co., one of the largest East India merchants, with debts of £3 million, was an entirely different matter. The Union Bank was the only Scottish bank involved, and this also affected other bank customers such as Alexander Dennistoun, Finlay Campbell & Co., and Smith Fleming & Co. Losses of £150,000 were sustained, which required a reduction of £120,000 in the bank's reserve and money to be earmarked from the 1876 profits. The Collie fraud seriously damaged both the Union Bank's business and its public image.

The events of 1878 and the City of Glasgow Bank affair gave a further downward twist to public confidence in the Union Bank. Gairdner, the general manager, with the full support of the bank's Edinburgh and Glasgow boards, issued the following statement:

> The Directors deem it right to make a Special Report to the Proprietors on the extent to which their interests have been affected by the suspension of the City of Glasgow Bank and subsequent failures, and this more particularly as four months must elapse before the Annual Meeting is held.
>
> The amount due to the Bank by the City of Glasgow Bank, exclusive of the Notes retired in the public interest, is only £4,000. These claims, it is believed, will be paid in full; and the Directors have the satisfaction of informing the Proprietors that, on a careful estimate of all other bad and doubtful debts, the provision required from the profits of the current year is under £3,700.

156   The Directors believe it will also be satisfactory to the Proprietors to receive at this time an explicit assurance that the Accounts of the Bank are closely and constantly scrutinized by them; that the Advances are safe and well distributed; that losses are invariably provided for as they arise; that the Securities and Investments are of greater value than they stand at in the Books; and that the Bank's Capital of £1,000,000, and Rest of £330,000 are intact. The Proprietors will have observed that an unusual fall has recently taken place in the market price of the Bank's Stock. In connection with this, it is right to mention that a considerable amount of the Stock offered for sale belongs to Proprietors who, unhappily for themselves, are involved as Shareholders in the City of Glasgow Bank. The Bank sustains no loss from this circumstance; and as sales are effected, this depressing influence will, no doubt, pass away.

The Directors have delayed issuing this Report until the effects of the commercial and financial disorder of October have been so far developed as to admit of the Board reporting with confidence on their bearing on the Bank.

The selling price of Union Bank stock stood at £270 in November 1875; a month later it was only £160, a figure at which it remained for most of the succeeding year. Two measures were taken to try to restore confidence. In 1879 a full external audit of the bank's affairs was undertaken and, when published, was on the whole favourably received. Only *The Economist* struck a sour note with a judgment which the 1995 business editor might endorse: 'a good set of accounts may exist with bad business'.

The most important step of all was that the bank took advantage of the Companies Act of 1879 to register, and thereby secured limited liability for its shareholders. One of Charles Gairdner's very strong beliefs was that where a bank had limited liability it should have a reserve capacity of capital immediately available to protect the note issue. Thus a special meeting called in February 1882 agreed to increase the nominal capital of the bank to £5 million, while the paid-up capital was to remain at £1 million.

In addition to difficulties created by the general conditions of the 1880s the Union Bank had a continuing problem with its share price and continued to lose out to the other Scottish banks in the proportion of its advances to its deposits. The geographical flow of business noted in Bank of Scotland was repeated almost exactly in the Union Bank. In most branches 30 to 40 per cent of deposits could be lent, and money flowed therefore to Glasgow and London. Throughout the whole period, the affairs of J. & G. Thomson required major nursing. In 1874 the firm had moved from its shipyard at Finnieston to new works at

Union Bank Office, George Street, Edinburgh, by David Bryce

Dalmuir, Clydebank. By 1881 the advances stood in the books at £124,000, but a bad fire and delay in commissioning put the firm's future in jeopardy. Careful examination of the books led to a restructuring of the firm, which was relaunched as a public company in 1889. The background against which Thomson's emerged in 1889 as the most modern yard on the Clyde, and Clydebank itself as a 'new' town, was the phenomenal growth in iron shipbuilding on the Clyde after 1860. In the 1880s mild steel replaced iron in hull construction, and Clydeside yards built one-third of all British merchant tonnage, which was 18 per cent of the world total. By 1885 the Union Bank had declined from second place to sixth in the ranking of Scottish banks and there can be little doubt therefore that Charles Gairdner's legacy was a mixed one. To the outsider he was a formidable intellectual figure who appeared to devote himself to writing papers on banking and economic subjects. Within the bank he was an austere, autocratic manager who increased the bank's investments and maintained a tight discipline on banking policy. His shortcomings as a banker are reflected in the fact that at his retiral in 1895 the advances of the Union Bank were the smallest in Scotland at precisely the time that Glasgow was developing into a world-class industrial centre.

From its establishment in December 1877 the Union Bank's London office became the main channel for translating deposits into profitable investment, mostly in colonial government or railway bonds.

Charles Gairdner's successor was Robert Blyth, who had been manager of the Scottish Amicable Life Assurance Society. He was general manager until 1910, when he retired. The most notable domestic change of these

158   years was the reconstruction of the Union's London office on the corner of Cornhill and Bishopsgate in the City of London. In 1910 Arthur C.D. Gairdner (nephew of Robert Blyth and grandson of Charles Gairdner) was appointed general manager, and in the four years before the outbreak of the First World War he began to develop new business and once again to increase the level of profitability. There was one innovation in those years for which the staff of the bank felt profoundly grateful. In 1911 the sum of £10,000 was applied to a pensions and allowances fund which was translated into a fully-fledged and funded pension and superannuation scheme. It was contributory, and from the outset included bank officers among the trustees.

	Glasgow and Union Bank	Thistle Bank	Sir William Forbes &	Paisley Union Bank	Hunters & Co., Ayr	Glasgow and Ship Bank	**Union Bank of Scotland**
	1836	1836	1838	1838	1843	1843	
paid-up capital	287,050	–	–	24,000	18,000	500,000	1,000,000
total liabilities	1,284,072	468,604	1,580,835	447,099	–	2,414,665	6,294,782
advances	480,812	213,088	824,057	137,233	–	1,789,799	4,669,414
reserve	1,344	3,300	91,500	–	–	50,030	100,000
profits	16,844	–	16,000	–	2,650	55,000	82,623
no. of partners	517	8	6	3	10	36	–
branches	14	–	4	5	8	3	29

Union Bank of Scotland £20 note of 31 March 1905